An Introduction to the
Psychology of Dreaming

An Introduction to the Psychology of Dreaming

Kelly Bulkeley

PRAEGER

Westport, Connecticut
London

Library of Congress Cataloging-in-Publication Data

Bulkeley, Kelly, 1962–
    An introduction to the psychology of dreaming / Kelly Bulkeley.
        p.   cm.
    Includes bibliographical references and index.
    ISBN 0–275–95889–2 (alk. paper).—ISBN 0–275–95890–6 (pbk. :
alk. paper)
    1. Dreams.   2. Dream interpretation.   3. Psychology.   I. Title.
BF1078.B78   1997
154.6′3—dc21   96–53613

British Library Cataloguing in Publication Data is available.

Library of Congress Catalog Card Number: 96–53613
ISBN: 0–275–95889–2 (hc)
        0–275–95890–6 (pb)

First published in 1997

Praeger Publishers, 88 Post Road West, Westport, CT 06881
An imprint of Greenwood Publishing Group, Inc.

Printed in the United States of America

For Lightning, Thunder, and Brownie

Contents

Acknowledgments

I would like to thank Sybe Terwee for introducing me to Greenwood Press and encouraging me to take on this project. Doug Daher, George Goethals, Don Browning, Bertram Cohler, and Peter Homans have my deep appreciation for being my most trusted guides in exploring the psychology of dreaming. Of the many dream researchers who over the past several years have been my teachers and friends, five of them—Ernest Hartmann, Johanna King, Carol Schreier Rupprecht, Alan Siegel, and Jeremy Taylor—have given especially valuable support during the writing of this book. The writings of Anthony Shafton and Robert Van de Castle have provided me with consistently excellent reference materials, and I recommend their books to readers who want further introductory perspectives on dream psychology. To Chris Altschuler I owe gratitude for regularly providing me with creative inspiration, existential companionship, and fashion tips. To Dr. Polly Young I give thanks for introducing me to Dientamoeba Fragilis, Endolimax Nana, and Blastocystis Hominis, my long-unknown intestinal cohabitants. Rex Marinaro, Joanne Rochon, and Matthew Christianson gave me their expert assistance in the final editing and design of the book. And to Hilary, Dylan, and Maya, thank you for everything.

Chapter 1

Three Basic Questions about Dreaming: Formation, Function, Interpretation

I went into a bookstore, like the Cottage bookstore on 4th Street in San Rafael. There were two people, I think, a man and a woman. The man, the proprietor of the place, offered me some money to kill a man out in back. I casually said sure, and wrote my name down in some sort of ledger. I went around, and shot a guy with a gun I had. I came back around, thinking about how much I should get paid. I wanted $100, but the man told me that I was going to get $25. When I signed my name, I had for some reason given the man a check for $8.00. Now I started to worry, and it seemed that the man I was dealing with was nervous too. I wanted to get away, but my name in the ledger was evidence of my being there, and I knew that the police would question me if I didn't do something. I tried to think how a purchase, plus tax, could equal exactly $8.00. I left, going up 4th Street on a bike, I think. It was dusk, and the street was deserted—no people or cars. I was really worried now, thinking first about all the different scenarios in which the police would catch me, and then second about how readily and nonchalantly I had killed that guy. I hadn't even thought about it before I did it, and now I was shocked at myself.

—Edward, 19-year old college student

Edward wakes up, and says that while he was asleep in his bed he felt like all these things were *really happening* to him; he felt like he was *really experiencing* these feelings, activities, and events. He says that certain images and emotions were extremely vivid—the strangely deserted street, the growing fear of the police, the sudden shock of realization that he'd killed the man behind the bookstore.

Edward recognizes that many details of the experience are directly related to aspects of his ordinary waking life. The bookstore is a place he has been visiting for years to buy books. Thinking about money, writing checks, and signing his name are all common, daily activities. But other details have no apparent connection to anything in his life. Edward has never been in a real fight before, let alone killed anyone. He has never before seen the man and woman in the bookstore, nor the man whom he shoots outside. The financial transactions are all very puzzling; Edward feels sure that the $100, $25, and $8 figures *mean* something, although he does not know what. The whole experience felt very real and somehow terribly meaningful. But Edward is at a loss to say what it was all about.

How do we make sense of such an experience? Is it possible to analyze it, explain it, understand it?

To begin with, we classify such an experience as a *dream*. We say that while Edward was asleep in his bed he was *dreaming*: he dreamed that he went into the bookstore, wrote his name in the ledger, went out and shot the man, and so forth.

But what, then, is a dream?

For thousands of years humans have been fascinated, intrigued, and perplexed by their dreams. People in cultures all over the world, through every period of history, have wondered what dreams are about. Some of the oldest written texts every discovered are devoted to describing and interpreting people's dreams.

Psychologists have naturally taken a deep interest in dreams. Psychology arose in the late eighteenth century as an academic discipline devoted to the application of scientific methodologies to the study of the psyche (a Greek term which is variously translated as "life," "spirit," "soul," "mind," "intellect"). Dreams, psychologists immediately recognized, are phenomena that offer a means to explore mental structures and processes that are inaccessible to normal waking awareness. By means of careful observation, experimentation, and research, psychologists have found that dreams reveal many important aspects of our mental world. The dynamics of personality, the workings of perception and memory, the interactions of reason and emotion, the complex relations between mental experiences and bodily functions—these are just some of the important subjects that psychologists have learned more about by studying dreams.

During the twentieth century the psychological investigation of dreams has expanded tremendously in both scope and sophistication. In the last one hundred years psychologists have used a variety of new methods and techniques for investigating dreams. They have studied different types and forms of dreaming experience, examined the relations of dreams to other psychological experiences and processes, and explored the various connections between dreaming life and waking life. The result of all this research has been nothing less than a revolution in how we view human nature. Anyone who wants to understand the essential qualities and the potentials for growth of the human mind must now take into account modern psychological research on the phenomenon of dreaming.

This book is an introduction to the twentieth century's major psychological theories about dreams and dreaming. It offers a history of how these theories have developed from 1900 to the present, and an extensive bibliography of key books and articles on modern dream research. Although the focus is specifically on the psychological study of dreams and dreaming, some attention will be given to approaches taken by other fields of study (e.g., anthropology, literature, religion).

Attention will also be given to the sociohistorical context of twentieth century psychology, and specifically to the influence of this context on why psychologists are interested in dreams, how they have studied dreams, and what they have discovered.

The major approaches to dreams and dreaming are presented here in a roughly chronological order, to give readers a sense of how each new approach depends (in complex and varying ways) on those approaches that preceded it. The work of Sigmund Freud is described first, in Chapter 2, as he gave the pioneering modern statement of a comprehensive psychology of dreaming. Freud developed an approach to dreams that every subsequent theory has had to acknowledge and respond to: the modern psychology of dreaming simply cannot be understood without a solid grounding in Freud's work. Next comes the dream theory of Carl Jung. Although originally a student of Freud, Jung split with Freud and went on to formulate his own approach to dreams. In many ways, Jung's work has become even more influential than Freud's on twentieth century dream psychology.

Chapter 4 discusses the many alternative clinical views of dreams that have developed out of the therapeutic practices of different psychologists. These approaches offered responses, revisions, and sometimes vigorous challenges to the theories of Freud and Jung. The fifth chapter outlines the body of psychophysiological research generated by the discovery of rapid eye movement sleep (REM sleep) in the 1950s by sleep laboratory researchers at the University of Chicago. This research indicated that the subjective mental experience of dreaming is closely related to complex physiological processes occurring in the brain during sleep. The sixth chapter describes the work of experimental psychologists, who have used scientifically rigorous methodologies to look at the relationship of dreaming to different processes of mental functioning (such as the development of reason, language, memory, imagination, and cognitive-emotional structures). In Chapter 7 the approaches of popular psychologists are examined. Special attention is given to their energetic efforts to "democratize" the study of dreams—to expand the practical applications of psychological theories about dreams and to make those theories more accessible to the general public.

Many different chronologies of the twentieth century psychology of dreaming could be constructed, of course. The goal of the particular chronology in *An Introduction to the Psychology of Dreaming* is to display as clearly as possible how each new psychological approach to dreams is related to those approaches that preceded it. If readers learn to recognize these often subtle and complex historical relationships, their understanding of the field as a whole will be greatly enhanced.

THREE BASIC QUESTIONS ABOUT DREAMING

Already it should be clear that the twentieth century psychology of dreaming is a remarkably diverse field of study. Anyone who wants to understand this field faces the daunting task of trying to make sense of all these different approaches. The greatest service an introductory book can render is to help readers in this process. *An Introduction to the Psychology of Dreaming* will try to give readers an integrated view of modern dream psychology by focusing its analysis on three basic questions.

The first question is, how are dreams *formed*? Consider Edward's dream, presented at the beginning of this chapter. How exactly was his experience created? How was such a vivid, lifelike experiential world generated in the first place? Given that it occurred while Edward was sleeping, how was the formation of the dream related to the special mental and physical conditions of being asleep? What role did Edward's faculties of reason play in forming the dream? At certain points in the dream Edward is self-aware, and he rationally reflects on his experiences just as he might do in waking life. But at other points bizarre, seemingly random events happen to him without his understanding or control. If the dream was not willed by Edward's waking consciousness, if it was essentially an involuntary experience, then what *did* cause it to happen?

The second basic question is, what *functions* do dreams serve? Is there a purpose or reason why Edward had this experience? Does his dream have any adaptive value, any evolutionary significance? Does it play some kind of constructive role in his mental functioning? If so, how could such values or roles be demonstrated? Are the possible functions of dreams related in any way to the more general functions of sleep? And what if Edward had not written his dream down when he woke up, but had simply forgotten it—would the experience still serve any important functions? Do dreams have to be consciously remembered and reflected upon to fulfill their functions?

The third basic question is, how can dreams be *interpreted*? Can dreams be understood as expressions of meaning? Does a given dream have one fundamental meaning, or many different meanings? Or are dreams essentially random non-sense, devoid of any meanings whatsoever? If dreams are assumed to be meaning-ful, what kind of techniques should be used to interpret them? For example, what kind of skills, methods, or special information would be required to interpret Edward's dream? Could Edward interpret his dream himself, or would he need help from someone else? Could someone interpret the dream without knowing anything about Edward? How would we know if an interpretation of his dream was correct? How would we know that an interpretation wasn't simply reading meanings into the dream that aren't really there? If two different interpretations were given for the same dream, could we say that one is better than the other? What criteria would we use to make such a judgment?

Every modern psychological approach to dreaming addresses these three basic questions. The distinct identity of each theory is clearly illustrated by its answers to these three questions. By carefully examining the answers given to these questions by twentieth century psychologists who have studied dreams, readers will be in a good position to evaluate the field as a whole—and then to formulate their own answers.

THE THREE BASIC QUESTIONS IN WESTERN HISTORY

Modern psychologists are not the first to ask about the formation, function, and interpretation of dreams. Many other people throughout history have investigated dreams, reflected on them, developed theoretical models to understand them, and utilized practical methods to apply them in various areas of daily life. A full account of dreams in human history is far beyond the scope of this book. But it is essential for readers to have some awareness of this long and rich history if they want to have a well-grounded understanding of twentieth century dream psychology. Such an historical awareness provides a helpful context in which to evaluate the approaches that modern psychologists have taken to the study of dreams and dreaming.

What follows are brief summaries of how dreams are explained and understood in three classic Western sources: the Bible, the philosophy of Aristotle, and the *Oneirocriticon* of Artemidorus.

The Bible

The Bible is filled with material on dreams: reports of dream experiences, examples of dream interpretations, and comments on the nature and function of dreams. However, this does not mean that a unified theory of dreams is presented in the Bible. The sixty-six books that make up the Old and New Testaments were written over the course of many centuries, by many different writers with often sharply differing theological views. These books were not collected into a single canonical text until the Vulgate Latin translation by Jerome in the early fifth century A.D. It would therefore be foolish to look for a single consistent line of reasoning about dreams across the many books of the Bible. Rather, the Bible offers a variety of different perspectives on dreams, and these complexly interrelated perspectives have had a huge influence on Western thought about the experience of dreaming.

The Bible presents dreams as one of the chief means by which God communicates with humans. A primary message conveyed by dreams in the Bible is simply God's immediate, vital presence in the life of the dreamer. This message is illustrated in Abram's experience of "a dread and great darkness" falling upon him (Gen. 15), Jacob's dream of the heavenly ladder (Gen. 28), Samuel's experience in the temple of the Lord (1 Sam. 3), and Solomon's dream at Gibeon (1 Kings 3). Beyond revealing God's numinous presence, many of the dreams also convey messages of reassurance, guidance, and counsel to the dreamers. For example, the book of Matthew describes three dreams experienced by Joseph, husband of Mary, that reassure him and help him lead his family to safety, away from the dangerous King Herod (Matt. 1–2). Similarly, Paul receives dreams from God that guide him in his missionary work, directing him to be faithful and go preach the gospel in certain needy lands (Acts 16, 18).

A few dreams in the Bible offer specific prophecies of what will happen in the future. Pharaoh's dream of the seven fat cows and seven lean cows, followed by a dream of seven plump ears of grain and seven thin ears of grain, together foretell a coming famine in Egypt (Gen. 41). Gideon overhears a dream described by a Midianite soldier that foretells the victory of Israel over its Midianite enemies (Judges 7). At times, dreams in the Bible are frightening, and serve as warnings to people. Jacob wrestles with a mysterious being until daybreak (Gen. 32), and Job suffers horrible nightmares (Job 7). Abimelech is warned in a dream not to touch Abraham's wife Sarah (Gen. 20), and the Babylonian King Nebuchadnezzar's nightmare warns him that he will be driven mad if he does not submit to God's rule (Dan. 4). While Pontius Pilate sits in judgment of Jesus, his wife says, "Have nothing to do with that righteous man, for I have suffered much over him today in a dream" (Matt. 27).

The Bible presents two detailed accounts of the practice of dream interpretation. In the first, Joseph interprets the dreams of the baker and the butler (Gen. 40) and of the Pharaoh (Gen. 41). Although Joseph explains in clear, rational terms what the particular images of their dreams mean (e.g., the seven fat and lean cows mean seven years of plentiful harvests followed by seven years of famine), he insists that dream interpretations "belong to God." Joseph says to Pharaoh, "It is not in me; God will give Pharaoh a favorable answer." In the second account, Daniel carefully interprets the dreams of King Nebuchadnezzar (Dan. 1–4). Like Joseph, Daniel explains the symbolic meaning of each image in Nebuchadnezzar's dreams (e.g., a great tree symbolizes the king himself) and says that his interpretive skills are due entirely to God's inspiration and guidance.

A very significant aspect of dreams in the Bible is their direct relevance to the broader community. The dreams address the concerns not just of the individual dreamer, but also of the community of God's faithful. When God appears to Solomon in a dream and asks what gift he would like, Solomon says, "Give thy servant therefore an understanding mind to govern thy people, that I may discern between good and evil; for who is able to govern this thy great people?" (1 Kings 3). Likewise, the dreams of Abram, Abimelech, the Midianite soldier, Jacob, Samuel, Joseph, and Paul all express God's care and concern for the welfare of the human community.

However, many passages in the Bible also express deep skepticism towards dreams. Dreams are portrayed in Numbers 12 as a potentially deceptive "dark speech," in contrast to the clear revelations of God's will enjoyed by a prophet like Moses. In the book of Ecclesiastes it is said, "For a dream comes with much business, and a fool's voice with many words" (Ecc. 5). Similarly, the book of Deuteronomy warns people not to believe those "dreamers of dreams" who promote the idolatrous worship of other gods (Deut. 13). The prophet Jeremiah rails against those who falsely claim to know of God's will through their dreams (Jer. 23). There is no naive, simpleminded acceptance in the Bible of *all* dreams as divine revelations. While some dreams may indeed disclose God's presence, other dreams are dismissed as vain illusions—"on awaking you despise their phantoms" (Ps. 73).

The Philosophy of Aristotle

The Greek philosopher Aristotle (384–322 B.C.), a student of Plato, analyzed dreams in two short treatises, *On Dreams* and *On Prophesying by Dreams*. Plato had discussed dreams in some of his dialogues, but he never focused on dreams as a particular object of inquiry. Aristotle, however, devotes these two brief works to an examination of dreams, and the views he expresses have had an enduring influence on Western conceptions of dreams (all the more so because his views were essentially restated and endorsed by the Catholic theologian Thomas Aquinas [1225–1274 A.D.] in his *Summa Theologica*).

In *On Dreams*, Aristotle starts with the observation that when we sleep our faculties of sense perception cease their normal operations; likewise, our intellectual faculties suspend their ordinary functioning during sleep. So dreams do not arise from sense perceptions or from the intellect, which Aristotle believes are the only faculties by which we acquire knowledge. He claims that dreams are caused by echoes of emotionally charged sense perceptions from our daily lives. When we go to sleep, the external objects that we perceive while awake leave the range of our senses; however, there are still impressions from these objects echoing within us, and those echoes themselves become new objects of perception. The problems begin, Aristotle says, when we fail to distinguish those internal echoes from the external objects, and this is precisely what happens in dreams. Aristotle says that dreams are especially liable to mislead us because of the role played in them by the emotions:

We are easily deceived respecting the operations of sense-perception when we are excited by emotions, and different persons according to their different emotions; for example, the coward when excited by fear, the amorous person by amorous desire; so that, with but little resemblance to go upon, the former thinks he sees the object of his desire; and the more deeply one is under the influence of the emotion, the less similarity is required to give rise to these illusory impressions. (Aristotle 1941a, 621)

These deceptive, emotionally charged sense perceptions make an even greater impact on us when we are asleep, Aristotle argues, because our ordinary faculties of reason are so diminished. However, he grants that at times our faculties of reason do indeed remain active while dreaming, "for often, when one is asleep, there is something in consciousness which declares that what then presents itself is but a dream" (Aristotle 1941a, 624).

In *On Prophesying by Dreams* Aristotle evaluates claims that dreams may be divine revelations that foretell the future. He is generally skeptical of such claims, because "it is absurd to combine the idea that the sender of such dreams should be God with the fact that those to whom he sends them are not the best and wisest, but merely commonplace persons" (Aristotle 1941b, 626). Nevertheless, Aristotle says that allegedly prophetic dreams can be regarded in three different ways. They may be *causes*, *tokens*, or *coincidences* (Aristotle 1941b, 626). Dreams may indeed be the cause of future actions, Aristotle argues, for matters of importance in our waking lives regularly appear in our dreams; and just as waking life matters can influence dreams, "conversely, it must happen that the movements set up first in sleep should also prove to be starting-points of actions to be performed in the daytime" (Aristotle 1941b, 627). He says that dreams may also be tokens of events to come in the future. He refers to dreams that reveal the imminent onset of an illness, before the person has become consciously aware of being sick. Aristotle says that in the quiet of sleep we become aware of slight movements and beginnings that are lost to us in the bustle of daily life; "[I]t is manifest," he says, "that these beginnings must be more evident in sleeping than in waking moments" (Aristotle 1941b, 627).

Having granted all this, Aristotle still believes that "most [so-called prophetic] dreams are, however, to be classed as mere coincidences," especially those that are extravagant, or that involve matters with no direct connection to the dreamer (Aristotle 1941b, 627). It happens all the time, he argues, that people mistakenly connect two events that are in fact unrelated. People make the same error when they connect a striking dream to a striking, but actually unrelated, event that comes after the dream.

Regarding the interpretation of dreams, Aristotle's analysis suggests that if we are able to recognize and account for the distorting influence of our emotions, then we may gain genuine and potentially valuable knowledge from our dreams. While dreaming we sometimes discover in those echoing sense perceptions important features of the world, features that we had overlooked in the busy activity of our waking life. Aristotle compares dreams to forms reflected in a pool of water: when the water is calm, the forms can be easily perceived; but when the water is troubled (i.e., when the mind is agitated by the emotions), the reflection becomes distorted and unintelligible. According to Aristotle, the trick to becoming a "skilful interpreter" is learning how to "rapidly discern, and at a glance comprehend, the scattered and distorted fragments of such forms" (Aristotle 1941b, 630). If we can develop this skill, which Aristotle defines as "the faculty of observing resemblances" (Aristotle 1941b, 630), we may learn something of value from our dreams.

The *Oneirocriticon* of Artemidorus

The *Oneirocriticon* (*Interpretation of Dreams*) of Artemidorus of Daldis is by far the longest, most detailed, and most sophisticated text on dreams to survive from ancient times. Artemidorus lived in the second century A.D., during a peaceful, prosperous era of the Roman empire. Few details of his life are known, beyond the facts that he was very well read and traveled widely throughout the Mediterranean world. But despite his relative anonymity, Artemidorus's book has profoundly influenced dream interpreters throughout Western history.

In the *Oneirocriticon* Artemidorus offers a manual for the practical interpretation of dreams. He refers to many other such manuals that he has read, indicating that there was a lively tradition of dream literature during this era. Indeed, Artemidorus makes a point of emphasizing that he has studied every book on dream interpretation he could find and that he has even "consorted for many years with the much-despised diviners of the marketplace" (Artemidorus 1975, 13). He goes on to say,

> People who assume a holier-than-thou countenance and who arch their eyebrows in a superior way dismiss them as beggars, charlatans, and buffoons, but I have ignored their disparagement. Rather, in the different cities of Greece and at great religious gatherings in that country, in Asia, in Italy and in the largest and most populous of the islands, I have patiently listened to old dreams and their consequences. For there was no other possible way in which to get practice in these matters. (13)

As this passage suggests, Artemidorus is keenly aware of the skepticism many people hold toward dream interpretation. He wrote the *Oneirocriticon* as a response to that skepticism, trying to demonstrate the legitimacy and practical value of dream interpretation in ordinary people's lives and experiences.

Artemidorus classifies dreams into various types. The first distinction he makes is between *enhypnion* and *oneiros*: "Oneiros differs from enhypnion in that the first indicates a future state of affairs, while the other indicates a present state of affairs" (14). As examples of enhypnion he describes hungry people dreaming of eating, thirsty people dreaming of drinking, and fearful people dreaming of what they fear. These dreams, Artemidorus says, merely reflect the present condition of the dreamer. Oneiros, by contrast, goes beyond the present to "call to the dreamer's attention a prediction of future events" (14).

The second distinction Artemidorus makes is between *theorematic* and *allegorical* dreams. Theorematic dreams are direct in their imagery and meaning. An example is a man who dreams of a shipwreck, and then in waking life the shipwreck actually happens, exactly as in the dream. Allegorical dreams use indirect imagery and symbolism to express their meanings: an example here would be a dream of returning from Hades, which might signify that the dreamer was going to return from a foreign land to his own country. Artemidorus says that through allegorical dreams, "the soul is conveying something obscurely by physical means" (15). Although he suggests in this passage, and elsewhere in his book, that the source of dreams lies in certain prophetic powers of the soul, Artemidorus declines to engage in debate on this point:

I do not, like Aristotle, inquire as to whether the cause of our dreaming is outside of us and comes from the gods or whether it is motivated by something within, which disposes the soul in a certain way and causes a natural event to happen to it. Rather, I use the word in the same way that we customarily call all unforeseen things god-sent. (20–21)

The main body of the *Oneirocriticon* is an extensive catalog of different dream images and their interpretations. For example, Artemidorus discusses dreams of going blind, of losing teeth, of being beheaded; dreams of various kinds of sexual behavior; dreams of rivers, mountains, clouds, and trees; dreams of kings, priests, gods, and mythological beasts; on and on and on, in remarkably minute and painstaking detail. According to Artemidorus, most dreams have significance for the personal life of the dreamer, relating to the dreamer's health, family, occupation, romantic relationships, and so forth. He does grant, though, that the dreams of some people (e.g., political leaders) may have significance for the broader community as well.

Some modern psychologists have accused Artemidorus of devising a kind of "cookie cutter" system of dream interpretation, in which each dream image is assigned a particular meaning regardless of the dreamer's personal life context. A close reading of the *Oneirocriticon* shows, however, that Artemidorus insists that any accurate dream interpretation must rely on a detailed knowledge of the dreamer's life: "It is profitable—indeed, not only profitable but necessary—for the dreamer as well as for the person who is interpreting that the dream interpreter know the dreamer's identity, occupation, birth, financial status, state of health, and age" (21). Artemidorus gives numerous examples in which the same dream dreamed by two different people can have two very different interpretations, depending on the particular life circumstances of the dreamers. Furthermore, although he goes to great lengths in the *Oneirocriticon* to teach his readers what he knows of the process of dream interpretation, Artemidorus insists that books are not enough: "I maintain that it is necessary for the interpreter of dreams to have prepared himself from his own resources and to use his native intelligence rather than simply to rely upon manuals" (22). Throughout the book he emphasizes that personal experience is the only reliable guide in the process of dream interpretation.

I have always called upon experience as the witness and guiding principle of my statements. Everything has been the result of personal experience, since I have not done anything else, and have always devoted myself, day and night, to the study of dream interpretation. (137)

CLASSIC WESTERN ANSWERS TO THE THREE BASIC QUESTIONS

The views on dreams expressed in the Bible, the philosophy of Aristotle, and the *Oneirocriticon* of Artemidorus can be analyzed in terms of the three basic questions of formation, function, and interpretation discussed above.

In the Bible, some dreams are formed directly by God, while other dreams seem to be merely the vain creations of the dreamer's own mind. Dreams serve a number of functions in the Bible: they can be divine revelations, expressions of reassurance and guidance, prophecies of the future, or warnings of possible danger. Dreams can be successfully interpreted by the use of certain symbolic translations from the dreams' imagery to their waking life analogs. The best interpreters, Joseph and Daniel, are guided first and foremost by their faith in God. However, the Bible also warns that some dreams can be meaningless and may be misinterpreted, thereby leading people into error and impiety.

In contrast to the Bible's portrait of dream revelations from God, Aristotle asserts that all dreams are formed by the dreamer's own sleep-impaired mind. Dreams have no real function, in Aristotle's view, beyond the small possibility of revealing perceptions of waking life that were overlooked during the day. He grants that dreams can be interpreted, in the sense that resemblances can be discerned between the distorted imagery of a dream and objects of waking life perception.

Artemidorus sidesteps the question of how dreams are formed; he is comfortable with either the idea that dreams are literally "god-sent" or the idea that dreams are caused by the human mind alone. Either way, Artemidorus believes that the valuable function of dreams is to foretell what will come in the dreamer's future. For Artemidorus, dreams are important messages that can be used to better the dreamer's waking life. To interpret dreams, Artemidorus instructs his readers to study all available texts on dreams, to learn as much as possible about the dreamer's personal life, and most of all to rely on one's own experience and native intelligence.

Brief as it has been, this review of how dreams have been regarded in three classic Western sources will hopefully give readers a historical context in which they can more fruitfully study and understand the twentieth century psychology of dreaming.

Chapter 2

Sigmund Freud Discovers "The Secret of Dreams"

A large hall—numerous guests, whom we were receiving.—Among them was Irma. I at once took her on one side, as though to answer her letter and to reproach her for not having accepted my "solution" yet. I said to her: "If you still get pains, it's really only your own fault." She replied: "If you only knew what pains I've got now in my throat and stomach and abdomen—it's choking me"—I was alarmed and looked at her. She looked pale and puffy. I thought to myself that after all I must be missing some organic trouble. I took her to the window and looked down her throat, and she showed signs of recalcitrance, like women with artificial dentures. I thought to myself that there was really no need for her to do that.—She then opened her mouth properly and on the right I found a big white patch; at another place I saw extensive whitish grey scabs upon some remarkable curly structures which were evidently modeled on the turbinal bones of the nose.—I at once called in Dr. M., and he repeated the examination and confirmed it. . . . Dr. M. looked quite different from usual; he was very pale, he walked with a limp and his chin was clean-shaven. . . . My friend Otto was now standing beside her as well, and my friend Leopold was perusing her through her bodice and saying: "She has a dull area low down on the left." He also indicated that a portion of the skin on the left shoulder was infiltrated. (I noticed this, just as he did, in spite of her dress.). . . M. said: "There's no doubt it's an infection, but no matter; dysentery will supervene and the toxin will be eliminated.". . . We were directly aware, too, of the origin of her infection. Not long before, when she was feeling unwell, my friend Otto had given her an injection of a preparation of propyl, propyls . . . propionic acid . . . trimethylamin (and I saw before me the formula for this printed in heavy type). . . . Injections of that sort ought not to be made so thoughtlessly. . . . And probably the syringe had not been clean.

> Sigmund Freud, July 23–24, 1895, in Freud
> 1965a, 139–41

Sigmund Freud analyzes and interprets this dream of his in Chapter 2 of *The Interpretation of Dreams* (1900 was the book's official publication date, although it actually first appeared in late 1899). The dream is now known as the "Dream of Irma's Injection" and also, because of its seminal importance in the development of Freud's theories, as "the specimen dream of psychoanalysis." Much of Freud's work relied directly on his own dreams and life experiences. To understand his work it is therefore essential to know something about his personal background. This chapter will start with a description of Freud's life up to the writing of *The Interpretation of Dreams*. It will then examine the dream theory that Freud presents in that book, and finally it will consider some of the additions, changes, and revisions Freud made later in his career to his dream theory. Although it has become fashionable in recent years to attack Freud for being outdated, unscientific, sexist, and the like, the fact remains that virtually all twentieth-century dream psychologists have derived their basic principles and techniques from Freud's revolutionary work.

Soon after *The Interpretation of Dreams* was published, Freud wrote a letter to his friend Wilhelm Fliess and described the house (a resort villa outside of Vienna) in which he had experienced his dream of Irma. Freud wrote, "Do you suppose that some day a marble tablet will be placed on the house, inscribed with these words?— 'In This House, on July 24th, 1895, the Secret of Dreams was Revealed to Dr. Sigm. Freud.' At the moment there seems little prospect of it" (1965a, 154). Although he did not live to see it, Freud's wish did come true. A marble plaque, inscribed with the exact words Freud had envisioned, was placed at the villa in 1977 (Masson 1985, 418).

FREUD'S LIFE

Sigismund Schlomo Freud was born in 1856 in Freiberg, Moravia, to Jacob Freud, a wool merchant, and his third wife Amalia.[1] As a child Freud was brought up in a rather complex network of family relations. Two sons from Jacob's first marriage lived nearby. One of them was older than Freud's relatively young mother Amalia, and the other was just a year younger than she. Freud's first playmate was his nephew—the little son of his oldest half-brother. In 1860 the family moved to Vienna, where Freud grew up and lived the whole of his life until 1938. The outbreak of World War II forced him to flee to London, where he died a year later, in 1939.

The Vienna of Freud's youth was an exciting place of optimism and opportunity. In 1867 Jews were officially granted political rights equal to those of other citizens and were increasingly accepted into mainstream society. Throughout his school years Freud, like many people in the Jewish community, followed the general trend towards cultural assimilation—he embraced the humanistic values of political liberalism, affirmed the universal goals of rationality and human freedom, and identified himself as a German rather than a Jew. But after 1880 the liberal political atmosphere abruptly evaporated. Anti-Semitism returned with a vengeance, and for young Jewish men like Freud, hopes for assimilation were suddenly shattered, replaced by deep disappointment and bitterness.

Freud entered the University of Vienna in 1873 and graduated in 1881 with a medical degree. From early childhood he had been deeply interested in scientific pursuits, and he found great pleasure in satisfying his natural curiosity by means of empirical research and investigation. Once out of school, though, Freud was forced to set aside his strong desire for a life of pure medical research. In the spring of 1882 Freud had met Martha Bernays, and within two months they were engaged. Freud quickly realized that private practice, not research, was the only realistic road to financial independence and the ability to provide an acceptable home for his fiancée. So over the next four years he slowly built up his medical practice by treating people suffering from hysteria, neuroses, and other mental disturbances. He continued to do as much research as he could, however, and he published several well-received scholarly articles on neurological disorders. Finally, in September of 1886, Sigmund and Martha got married. Between 1887 and 1895 they had a total of six children together.[2]

In 1896 his father died, and the loss pained Freud deeply. He spoke of his sufferings in his numerous letters to Wilhelm Fliess, the ear and nose specialist from Berlin who was Freud's closest friend during those years. In his letters Freud poured out his emotions, memories, confidences, dreams, anxieties, and wishes, as well as his latest psychological speculations. He told Fliess of the various physical ailments and neurotic symptoms that had been plaguing him, and he confessed that "the chief patient I am preoccupied with is myself" (Masson 1985, 261).

Early in 1898 Freud mentioned to Fliess that he had begun writing a book on dreams. By the fall of 1899 he had completed it, and he sent a copy to Fliess. Freud anxiously wrote, "I have long since become reconciled to [the book] and await its fate in—resigned suspense" (Masson 1985, 380).

THE INTERPRETATION OF DREAMS

In the preface to the second edition of *The Interpretation of Dreams* Freud admitted that his book had great personal significance for him. Looking back on the process of writing it, he found that it was "a portion of my own self-analysis, my reaction to my father's death—that is to say, to the most important event, the most poignant loss, of a man's life" (1965a, xxvi). Farther along in his career, when he struggled with doubts about his theories, Freud said that he always regained his confidence by turning back to *The Interpretation of Dreams*. And in 1930, when he reflected on his life's many achievements, he concluded that this book contained "the most valuable of all the discoveries it has been my good fortune to make. Insight such as this falls to one's lot but once in a lifetime" (1965a, xxxii). More than just a statement of his psychological theories, *The*

Interpretation of Dreams is a work that expresses Freud's most deeply held feelings and beliefs.

Freud's Method of Interpretation

At the outset of the book Freud announces his goals: to explain the origins of dream images, to understand the relationship of dreams to other abnormal mental phenomena (like phobias, obsessions, and delusions), and to develop new techniques for treating mental illness. Freud declares that while other psychological researchers have dismissed dreams as the nonsensical products of a sleep-impaired mind, he is going to demonstrate that dreams *do* have psychological meaning and *can* be interpreted.

Two popular methods of interpreting dreams have come down to us through history, Freud says. The first is the symbolic method, which takes the whole dream as a symbolic analogy for a waking life situation. As an example of this method Freud cites Joseph's interpretations of Pharaoh's dreams in the Bible. The second is the decoding method, in which a dictionary or manual is used to translate each part of a dream into a known meaning. Freud points to Artemidorus as practicing this method of interpretation. Freud says that both of these traditional methods are arbitrary, subjective, and essentially superstitious. But he insists that modern psychologists are wrong to dismiss dreams as a subject of serious scientific inquiry. Freud says that he agrees with the popular traditions that dreams are, if properly interpreted, profoundly meaningful expressions: "I must affirm that dreams really have a meaning and that a scientific procedure for interpreting them is possible" (1965a, 132).

Freud's approach to dream interpretation is similar to the decoding method in that it breaks the dream down into parts and analyzes the meaning of each specific image. But unlike the decoding method, Freud does not translate the dream's images according to the definitions prescribed in an interpreter's manual. Rather, he looks at what occurs to the *dreamer* in relation to each part of the dream. Freud asks the dreamer to "free associate"—to describe whatever thoughts come up in connection to the dream images, no matter how random, foolish, or embarrassing the thoughts might seem. The spontaneous ideas, feelings, and memories that emerge during free association are, Freud claims, the essential clues to the underlying meaning of the dream.

The Dream of Irma's Injection

Freud demonstrates this method by looking at his "Dream of Irma's Injection." Freud examines this dream very carefully, image by image, and he ponders the meaning of the various thoughts that come to his mind in connection with each element. As he goes on, he notices a recurrent theme beginning to appear: the dream presents a number of different explanations for Irma's pains. First it's "her own fault" for not listening to Freud; then her pains are apparently due to some physical disease; and then her troubles are caused by the "dirty syringe." In waking life, Irma was in fact a patient of Freud's, and he had been only partly successful in curing her illness. Some of Freud's medical colleagues (represented in the dream by Otto and Dr. M.) knew of the case, and Freud worried that they blamed him for Irma's persistent sufferings. But the dream portrays Freud as utterly blameless: in the dream Irma's pains are not Freud's fault, but are caused by a variety of other things.

At the end of his analysis Freud concludes that the dream shows how he *wishes* things were: he wishes he were blameless for Irma's pains. The motive for having the dream was this wish, and the dream represents the wish as fulfilled. This, Freud says, is the essence of dreams. This is the secret that was revealed to him at that house in 1895: *dreams are the fulfillments of wishes*.

Manifest and Latent Contents

The immediate objection to Freud's argument is, but what about nightmares? How could a terrifying dream filled with fear and anxiety possibly be the fulfillment of a wish?

Freud responds by saying that we must distinguish between the *manifest* and the *latent* contents of dreams. The manifest content is the surface of the dream, the images that we remember when we awaken. Underlying the dream's surface is the latent content, the deeper thoughts and feelings that Freud says are always expressions of wishes. When a dream is created the latent content becomes transformed in such a way that the underlying wish is heavily distorted, thus masking its original nature. This process of distortion, or *censorship*, is necessary because the latent wishes are often immoral or antisocial, relating to our basic sexual, aggressive, and egotistical instincts (in *The Interpretation of Dreams* Freud makes his original statement about the Oedipus complex, the tremendously powerful but deeply unconscious yearning in all men to kill their fathers and sleep with their mothers [Freud 1965a, 281–301]). He offers a few examples of dreams whose wishes are obvious in the manifest content (e.g., children's dreams and dreams of "convenience," in which a hungry person dreams of eating, or a thirsty person dreams of drinking). However, such obvious dreams are rare, and generally dreams do disguise their wishes. Freud always denied the popular misunderstanding of his theory that all dreams are motivated by sexual wishes. He says that while sexual wishes do indeed express themselves in dreams, other wishes appear as well. (1965a, 194, 432).

In his dream of Irma, the latent content involves deeply self-centered wishes that Freud felt were socially unacceptable. Such wishes are taken by a part of the psyche Freud calls the "censoring agency" and transformed in such a way that their immoral nature is hidden.

So one explanation Freud gives for the occurrence of nightmares is that fright-ening dreams do indeed fulfill wishes: the fear is created by the failure of the censoring agency to mask the wishes well enough. Nightmares are dreams in which the censor's defenses buckle, and the immoral wish succeeds in breaking through during sleep. Freud also offers a second explanation for frightening dreams. He says that many people have "a masochistic component in [their] sexual constitution," a sense of pleasure in being hurt or humiliated (1965a, 192). For such people, a terribly unpleasant dream could well be fulfilling a wish, a *maso-chistic* wish.

Freud notes one more possible explanation for why a dream might not appear to be the fulfillment of a wish. He recalls a patient to whom he had explained his theory of dreams. The next day she reported to him a dream of going on vacation with her mother-in-law. In waking life his woman strongly disliked her mother-in-law and had recently decided to go on vacation by herself. The dream, then, reverses the positive solution she had just reached; it seems to be the exact opposite of what the woman truly wished. The woman challenged Freud, insisting that her dream proved that his theory was wrong. After a moment's pause, Freud responded that the wish motivating her dream was exactly this, *to prove him wrong*. Freud noted that around the time of the woman's dream he had inferred that she must have suffered an earlier psychological trauma that was partly responsible for her current illness. At first the woman disputed this, but later admitted that Freud was right. Her dream was thus motivated by a very deep and powerful wish that Freud would be wrong, that that earlier trauma had never happened (1965a, 185). Freud goes on to say that readers of his book may have similar "counter-wish dreams," which will apparently disprove Freud's dream theory but will in fact stem from the wish that his theory about the sexual, aggressive, and egotistical instincts found in all humans not be true.

On the basis of this analysis of unpleasant feelings in dreams, Freud gives the following definition of the nature of dreams: "A dream is a (disguised) fulfillment of a (suppressed or repressed) wish" (1965a, 194).

The Dream Work

Looking more carefully at how latent wishes are transformed into the manifest content of the dream, Freud says that two basic sources are used in this process. One source is the "day residue," neutral or indifferent memories from regular day-to-day life. Recent images of ordinary activities are used in dreams as highly effective masks for underlying wishes—like "the sheep's clothing that hides the wolf" (1965a, 216). The other source of material for this process is more distant memories from the dreamer's past. Such recollections reach back to the earliest childhood expressions of those powerful instinctual wishes. The deeper the analysis of a dream goes, Freud claims, the closer one comes to the "track of experiences in childhood" which run throughout the dream's latent content.

The process of transformation itself Freud calls "the dream-work." Freud says that dreams are not, strictly speaking, creative or original in their formation. They are simply a reworking of material already in the psyche. The "essence" of the dream, then, is the dream-work, and not the latent wishes and thoughts which have been transformed by it (1965a, 179, 544–545). He describes four specific dream-work mechanisms that change latent thoughts, wishes, and memories into the manifest images of the remembered dream.

The first dream-work mechanism is *condensation*. Freud notes that sometimes the interpretation of a very simple dream image leads to a whole array of complex meanings. What happens, Freud says, is that the dream image serves as a "nodal point" at which many different latent thoughts converge. Looking at another one of his own dreams, the "Dream of the Botanical Monograph," Freud finds that a single dream image—looking through a book he has written—reveals, upon analysis, many different meanings: the dream image relates to a book he had in fact once written, and to a recent day's memory, and to his relationship with a colleague, and to his wife's personal likes and dislikes, and to a particular scene from his childhood. All of these latent thoughts are condensed into the manifest dream image of looking through the book. The mechanism of condensation is most clearly evident in dreams with characters that combine the features of two different people (e.g., the face of one person with the hair of another person), or with settings that combine details of two or more different places (e.g., a house from one place set in a different city or neighborhood). Freud found in analyzing his "Dream of Irma's Injection" that the character of Irma represented in condensed form a total of eight different women.[3] Freud says that such dream images are "overdetermined"—they contain a multitude of different and complexly-related meanings.

Displacement is the second dream-work mechanism. People often wonder why the emotions they feel in dreams are so often out of sync with what actually happens in the dream. For example, a trivial little incident in a dream might make a person cry hysterically, or flee in terror, or explode in anger. Freud explains these kinds of dreams by saying that the dream-work frequently shifts emotions associated with a particular latent thought or wish to a seemingly unrelated dream image. This displacement of emotional intensity is yet another way that the dream's latent content is masked: the feelings of sadness, fear, or anger that appear in the dream are not really connected to that trivial manifest image, but are in fact connected to certain repressed thoughts and wishes in the latent content. In such dreams the center of emotional intensity has been moved from its original place to a seemingly unimportant location within the dream (although Freud notes that his dream of Irma's injection does not shift the center of emotional intensity in this way (1965a, 341)).

The third mechanism of the dream-work is what Freud calls the *considerations of representability*. Because dreams are primarily visual experiences, Freud says a major part of the dream-work process involves transforming latent thoughts and wishes into visual images. One example of this would be a dream of a king and queen, which would visually represent latent thoughts about masculine and feminine powers. Another example would be a dream of being chased by a monster, which would visually represent latent thoughts about a frighteningly strong instinctual urge. Freud acknowledges that it is often very difficult to translate a dream's visual images back into the original latent content, but he insists that this difficulty is due to the psychological resistance people feel toward the deeply disturbing wishes underlying their dreams. In fact, the dream-work's goal is just this, to prevent those wishes from entering people's awareness. Dreams, Freud says, "are not made with the intention of being understood" (1965a, 377). This explains why we remember so few of our dreams—we don't want to remember them, we resist them.

In the course of representing the latent content in visual images the dream-work makes extensive use of symbols drawn from the popular culture of dreamer's social world. Male genitals may be represented in dreams by images of knives, guns, sticks, towers, snakes, and any other long, pointed object. Female genitals may be symbolized by images of boxes, ovens, rooms, ships, and vessels of various kinds. Symbols of sexual intercourse include flying, climbing stairs, and any image of up-and-down or back-and-forth movements. Freud notes that these same symbols appear abundantly in mythology, folklore, proverbs, and jokes. In some cases, then, he says the interpreter of a dream can go outside the dreamer's personal associations and find clues to the dream's latent meanings by referring to these common cultural symbols.

The fourth and final dream-work mechanism is *secondary revision*. Secondary revision works to smooth over the rough edges of the manifest dream. It fills in the gaps, makes minor revisions and additions, and generally gives the manifest dream a more orderly appearance. A common instance of this mechanism's work is revealed when a person tries to describe the connection between two different dream scenes. The person might say, "First I was in my home, and then I must have flown, or something like that, to a beach." What has happened, Freud says, is that two different dream scenes have been made to seem connected. By adding in the vague notion of flying, the dream-work has transformed the two scenes into one dream. This effort to create order and coherence links the dream-work mechanism of secondary revision with the activities of waking thought. Just as people seek order and coherence in their waking perceptions, so do they in dreams. Despite the connotations of its name, Freud insists that this fourth dream-work mechanism does not operate after the others have created the dream. Rather, secondary revision works directly on the latent dream material, right alongside the other dream-work mechanisms (although many years later Freud says that secondary revision occurs once the other dream-work mechanisms have finished performing their functions [1965b, 19–20]). And like those other mechanisms, secondary revision helps to disguise the latent meanings of the dream by strengthening the deceptive facade of the manifest dream. Freud mentions the extreme example of dreams in which the dreamer suddenly thinks, "This is only a dream." Freud says such "dreams within a dream" occur when the censoring agency has failed, and a forbidden wish has broken through. The very rational thought "this is only a dream" diminishes the importance of the dream—and thus fulfills the wish that what has just been dreamed *didn't happen* (1965a, 373–374).

Freud's Model of the Psyche

In the final chapter of *The Interpretation of Dreams* Freud discusses what dreams reveal about the fundamental nature of the human psyche. Having investigated the complex operations of the censoring agency and the four mechanisms of the dream-work, Freud concludes that the "mental apparatus" is composed of three "systems": consciousness, the preconscious, and the unconscious. Consciousness functions to perceive and process information from both external and internal sources. The preconscious system involves mental operations and processes that are not currently in the field of consciousness but could easily enter awareness if given attention. The unconscious system includes those instincts, wishes, memories, and other mental processes that have been repressed or denied access to the conscious and preconscious systems because of their deeply unsettling nature.

The formation of dreams, in what is known as Freud's "topographical" model of the psyche, can be explained as follows. When we fall asleep, a conflict soon arises between two different desires: on the one hand, we need the rest that peaceful sleep brings us; on the other, various unconscious urges take advantage of the weakened power of consciousness in sleep to assert themselves. But those urges are so immoral that they threaten to disrupt the person's sleep. So, in order to accommodate both the wish to sleep and the wish to satisfy unconscious urges, the mind (the "psychic apparatus") creates dreams as a compromise. The unconscious urges are transformed by the four mechanisms of the dream-work and are allowed a disguised, hallucinatory fulfillment that prevents their real nature from disturbing sleep. Dreams, Freud says, function as "the guardians of sleep" (1965a, 267).

Ultimately, what the psychological study of dreams reveals is the operation of two fundamentally different modes of human psychological functioning. Freud calls them the *primary process* (generally unconscious) and the *secondary process* (generally preconscious and conscious). Primary process thought is instinctual, wishful, irrational; its sole concern is to seek pleasure. In contrast, secondary process thought is sober, controlled, rational; its works to regulate the fulfillment of instinctual wishes in accordance with the demands of reality. Primary process thought is infantile, and interested in nothing beyond the individual's own wishes and desires. Secondary process thought is mature, and aware of the social and physical limits on satisfying those deeper instincts. The thoughts of children, primitives, and people with mental illnesses are governed by the primary process; the thoughts of sane modern adults are governed by the secondary process.

So the "core of our being," in Freud's view, consists of unconscious wishful impulses, of primary process yearnings for pleasure. Secondary process modes of thought develop later, and they help us channel those wishful impulses in more effective ways, by means of clear, rational perceptions of reality. Freud believes that this psychological development of ever greater secondary process control over the primary process occurs in each individual's growth from childhood to adulthood and also in the human race's growth from primitive to modern civilization. A later term Freud uses for this process of channeling and controlling is *sublimation*.

As helpful as dream interpretation may be in treating people with mental illnesses, Freud argues that the greatest value of interpreting dreams lies in the profound insights it gives into the fundamental nature of the human psyche. For this reason he declares that *"the interpretation of dreams is the royal road to a knowledge of the unconscious activities of the mind"* (1965a, 647). Freud says that dreams do not give us any knowledge about the future, at least in the sense that ancient peoples have always believed. Rather, dreams give us greater knowledge of the *past*, both of the dreamer's childhood and of humankind's primal stages of psychological development. Freud concludes his book by granting that perhaps dreams can be said to lead us into the future—by expressing those powerful and indestructible wishes that do indeed motivate all our life's activities and achievements.

FREUD'S LATER WRITINGS ON DREAMS

Over the next forty years of his life Freud made no fundamental changes to his dream theory. He repeatedly said that nothing had ever persuaded him to alter the basic principles laid out in *The Interpretation of Dreams*. However, he did make dozens of small additions and editorial revisions to the book, as a general effort to keep it up to date with new developments in dream research. And in his later writings he addressed two subjects that were not directly examined in *The Interpretation of Dreams*: post-traumatic dreams and telepathic dreams.

Post-Traumatic Dreams

In his 1920 work *Beyond the Pleasure Principle* Freud introduced a new view of the psyche, what is often called the "second topography" or the "structural model of the mind" (Gedo and Goldberg 1973). In this new view the psyche is made up of three "agencies": the *id*, the source of our instinctual energies and desires; the *superego*, the source of internal judgment, criticism, and morality; and the *ego*, which struggles to reconcile the demands of the id and the superego and to adapt the person's desires to the necessities of reality.

Freud developed this new "structural" model of id-superego-ego in part because the earlier topographical model of unconscious-preconscious-consciousness did not adequately explain post-traumatic dreams. People who have suffered a terrible trauma recently (e.g., in wartime combat) or in the distant past (e.g., in early childhood) frequently have recurrent dreams that directly replay the traumatic experience, with all the extremely fearful emotions that came with it. Such dreams, Freud realized, did not make sense in terms of the wish-fulfillment theory—what wish could possibly be satisfied by these terrible recurrent nightmares?

Freud acknowledged that traumatic dreams are not fulfilling any instinctual wish for pleasure. Rather, he decided that such dreams are motivated by a wish for mastery, a wish that reflects a more reality-based effort to overcome and control the anxiety arising from the traumatic event. These dreams express a wish not of the id, but of the ego. Freud's new structural model of the psyche allowed him to distinguish dreams generated by purely instinctual wishes (coming from the id) from dreams created in the service of waking life adaptation (coming from the ego). Post-traumatic dreams, then, are the only exceptions that Freud admits to his theory that dreams fulfill repressed instinctual wishes.

Telepathic Dreams

In a number of his later writings Freud examined the question of whether telepathy is possible in dreams (1953a, 1953b, 1953c, 1965b). Freud was generally suspicious toward all claims to occult knowledge because they appeared to him to be nostalgic efforts to revive religious superstitions in the face of modern scientific progress. Nevertheless, he insisted that telepathy should be investigated like any other phenomenon to determine if it could be empirically verified. So what does a scientific examination reveal about telepathy, the alleged extrasensory perception of other people's thoughts or far-distant events?

Freud studied a number of instances of telepathy in both waking and sleeping states, and he found that many of them could be accounted for by ordinary psychological operations of perception and reasoning. But other cases could not be so easily explained, and here Freud granted that genuinely telepathic, extrasensory modes of perception might be at work. He said that sleep seems to provide an especially good setting for such extrasensory perceptual modes to operate, and the information they convey is transformed by the dream-work just like any other latent content material. While scientists may not yet fully understand how telepathy operates, Freud argued that there is no reason to deny that it exists, nor to be frightened by it: "in my opinion it shows no great confidence in science if one does not think it capable of assimilating and working over whatever may perhaps turn out to be true in the assertions of occultists" (1965b, 49).

FREUD'S ANSWERS TO THE THREE BASIC QUESTIONS

Freud's answers to the three basic questions about dreams, posed in Chapter 1, can be summarized in this way:

Formation

During sleep, unconscious urges, wishes, and thoughts rise up to seek expression and fulfillment. Because this unconscious material is generally immoral and antisocial (relating to sexual, aggressive, and egotistical desires), it threatens to disrupt the individual's ability to sleep restfully. So the unconscious material is halted by a censoring agency in the psyche and transformed by the four mechanisms of the dream-work (condensation, displacement, considerations of representability, and secondary revision). What results is a deceitful manifest dream, put together out of bits and pieces of thoughts, memories, cultural symbols, and so forth, that has no apparent connection to the latent wishes and thoughts underlying it. Freud compares a dream's formation to the way that elaborate new facades were built over ancient Italian churches—the church's public front served as a mask to hide the original structure lying behind.

Function

In Freud's view dreams serve two important functions. One is to protect sleep, to allow the psychic apparatus to rest peacefully. The other is to provide a partial fulfillment, in hallucinated form, of those powerful unconscious urges, wishes, and desires that rise up during sleep. By gaining some measure of satisfaction through dreams, those unconscious forces put less pressure on waking consciousness; this helps people function more effectively in their daily lives. (In the exceptional case of people who have suffered extreme traumas, their dreams may serve the ego-related function of mastering anxiety and thus adapting better to reality.)

Interpretation

Dreams are not meant to be understood, Freud says. On the contrary, they are meant to deceive, to hide their true meanings from the dreamer. Furthermore, people actively resist understanding their dreams because those true meanings are so disturbing. Nevertheless, Freud argues that dreams can be interpreted, by a process of reversing the dream-work: by tearing down the dream's manifest facade, breaking it into pieces, and carefully reconstructing the original thoughts and wishes that motivated the dream's formation. An interpretation of a dream should begin by asking the dreamer to free associate to each image of the dream, describing whatever ideas, feelings, and memories spontaneously arise in connection with those images. At certain points the interpreter may go outside the dreamer's free associations and rely on the meanings of common cultural symbols to explain particular dream images. Dream interpretation has both practical and theoretical value for Freud. Practically, it aids in the treatment of mentally disturbed people. Theoretically, it gives valuable insights into the fundamental nature of the human psyche.

NOTES

1. Peter Gay notes that "the names that his father inscribed for him in the family Bible, 'Sigismund Schlomo,' did not survive Freud's adolescence. He never used 'Schlomo,' his paternal grandfather's name, and after experimenting with 'Sigmund' during his later years at school, adopted it some time after he entered the University of Vienna in 1873" (1988, 4–5).

2. Gay suggests that their long engagement, during which time both Freud and his fiancée appear to have been celibate, generated a high degree of sexual tension in Freud; and "those more than four interminable years of waiting left their imprint on the formation of Freud's theories about the sexual etiology of most mental ailments" (1988, 38).

3. The eight women represented in the dream are Irma herself, the governess, Irma's friend, Freud's wife, Freud's daughter Mathilda, the sulphonal patient named Mathilda, Freud's patient with nasal septal necrosis, and the 80-year old woman Freud gave morphine injections.

Chapter 3

C.G. Jung Descends into the Collective Unconscious

In the dream I was in [a] meadow. Suddenly I discovered a dark, rectangular, stone-lined hole in the ground. I had never seen it before. I ran forward curiously and peered down into it. Then I saw a stone stairway leading down. Hesitantly and fearfully, I descended. At the bottom was a doorway with a round arch, closed off by a green curtain. It was a big, heavy curtain of worked stuff like brocade, and it looked very sumptuous. Curious to see what might be hidden behind, I pushed it aside. . . . On [a] platform stood a wonderfully rich golden throne. . . . It was a magnificent throne, a real king's throne in a fairy tale. Something was standing on it which I thought at first was a tree trunk twelve to fifteen feet high and about one and a half to two feet thick. It was a huge thing, reaching almost to the ceiling. But it was of a curious composition: it was made of skin and naked flesh, and on top there was something like a rounded head with no face and no hair. On the very top of the head was a single eye, gazing motionlessly upward. . . . The thing did not move, yet I had the feeling that it might at any moment crawl off the throne like a worm and creep toward me. I was paralyzed with terror. At that moment I heard from outside and above me my mother's voice. She called out, "Yes, just look at him. That is the man-eater!"

C.G. Jung, age 3–4, in Jung 1965, 11–12

C.G. Jung is, besides Freud, the most influential dream psychologist of the twentieth century. Jung was for many years Freud's closest friend and leading student. But they had a bitter falling out (in part over their disagreement about the nature of dreams), and from that point on their respective theories developed in sharply different directions. Although zealous Freudians and Jungians battle each other to this day, most dream researchers recognize that both Freud and Jung were deeply insightful and creative psychological pioneers whose works have enduring relevance to the study of dreams.

Like Freud, Jung developed his psychological theories directly out of his own personal dream experiences. In his autobiography *Memories, Dreams, Reflections* (1965) he says that his intellectual life originated in the process of pondering his dreams. The dream quoted above is the earliest Jung could remember, one that never stopped haunting him. Throughout his life Jung experienced powerful dreams that inspired, shaped, and guided his psychological research.

As *Memories, Dreams, Reflections* makes clear, Jung's personal life and professional work were intimately connected.[1] This chapter will begin by describing some key aspects of Jung's life—his childhood dreams, his relationship with Freud, and his "confrontation with the unconscious." Then it will outline the basic elements of his theory of dreams and relate that theory to his general model of psychological development.

JUNG'S LIFE

Carl Gustav Jung was born in 1875 in a small village near Basel, Switzerland. He was brought up in a sternly Protestant household—his father, Paul, was a country parson and his mother, Emilie, was a minister's daughter. The gloomy religious atmosphere at home, combined with the various physical ills that afflicted everyone in the family, led the young Carl to become absorbed in his own private games, fantasies, and dreams. Jung says that his dream of the frightening "man-eater" in the cave showed him that the Lord Jesus wasn't the only power in the universe: "Through this childhood dream I was initiated into the secrets of the earth" (1965, 15). The religion of his father could not explain the occurrence of such strange dreams and visions, so Jung gradually developed the idea that there were two personalities living within him—personality number 1, the Swiss schoolboy and son of his parents; and personality number 2, an older, wiser, very mysterious man who came from the distant past.

As he got older Jung decided to study medicine, as a compromise between personality 1's interest in scientific knowledge and personality 2's fascination with the mysteries of nature. He soon focused on psychiatry and in 1900 took a post at the Burholzli Mental Hospital in Zurich. These, Jung says, were "the years of my apprenticeship" (1965, 114). The basic challenge of his work at the hospital was to discover what was going on inside his mentally ill patients. He listened carefully to their fantasies, dreams, and hallucinations, and he gradually realized that his patients were not "crazy" but were in fact struggling to answer fundamentally spiritual questions about the meaning of life. Traditional religious symbols, dogmas, and institutions had failed these people, leaving them helpless against external traumas and internal conflicts. Over the years Jung developed various therapeutic techniques to help his patients find, within their own unconscious selves, new symbols and truths that could relieve their sufferings.

In 1906 Jung, who had read *The Interpretation of Dreams* soon after it was published, sent a complimentary copy of his book on word associations to Freud. Freud wrote back a note of thanks, and soon the two were corresponding regularly. They met face-to-face for the first time in 1907, and according to Jung they "talked virtually without a pause for thirteen hours" (1965, 149). An intense and deeply ambivalent friendship had begun, one that would have a lifelong impact on both men. Jung quickly became Freud's most energetic and dedicated supporter, and Freud soon began referring to Jung as his chosen successor to lead the onward expansion of the psychoanalytic movement. Jung wrote articles promoting Freud's theories, helped to edit psychoanalytic journals, and worked on building up international organizations of Freud's followers.

But Jung says that from the start of their friendship he had uncomfortable feelings about Freud's emphasis on sexuality and his skepticism toward religion. As Jung began writing a new book, *Symbols of Transformation*, which challenged Freud on these points, he worried that their friendship would not survive the book's publication. Jung was right: When the work appeared in 1912 Freud felt betrayed by the person who was supposed to carry psychoanalysis victoriously into the future. Their letters to each other became increasingly angry, indignant, and scornful. By 1914 Jung and Freud broke off all relations with each other.

Now began what Jung called "a period of inner uncertainty," and what some of his biographers interpret as a "creative illness" (Ellenberger 1970, Homans 1979). His violent break with Freud led to a general withdrawal from the professional world. Jung resigned from all psychoanalytic associations, stopped reading scientific books and articles, and gave up his teaching position at the University of Zurich. For the next several years he was besieged by strange thoughts, visions, and dreams that he felt dreadfully incapable of understanding; "I stood helpless before an alien world" (1965, 177). Despite the pain and confusion he was experiencing, Jung decided to surrender to these unconscious impulses erupting within him and do his best to make sense of them. He regarded these years of "confrontation with the unconscious" as a scientific experiment, as an investigation into the darkest depths of the individual psyche. He allowed himself to play childish games, wrote out all his dreams and fantasies in exhaustive detail, and made elaborate drawings and paintings of especially haunting images. Using his family and his work at the hospital as anchors in social reality, Jung slowly learned to differentiate himself from these powerful images erupting out of the unconscious. This enabled him to bring them into relationship with his consciousness.[2]

This long inner crisis had come to a close by 1918, and what followed was "the Work"—Jung's major psychological writings. He took the dream and fantasy experiences of 1912–1918 as the "*prima materia*" for all his later research and theorizing: "it has taken me virtually forty-five years to distill within the vessel of my scientific work the things I experienced and wrote down at that time" (Jung 1965, 199). His psychological theories were devoted to communicating in scientific language what he had learned from the unconscious material that flooded through him during the years that followed his break with Freud.[3]

JUNG'S THEORY OF DREAMS

Jung did not write one great, systematic work on dreams, comparable to Freud's *The Interpretation of Dreams*. Rather, he discussed dreams in nearly everything he wrote, from *Two Essays on Analytical Psychology* (the first major work following his 1912–1918 crisis) to his final testament in *Memories, Dreams, Reflections*. The basic elements of his dream theory can be summarized as follows.

The Naturalness of Dreams

In Jung's view dreams are the direct, natural expression of the current condition of the dreamer's inner world. Jung rejects Freud's claim that dreams intentionally disguise their meanings, and he dismisses the psychoanalytic distinction between a dream's manifest and latent contents. Jung believes that dreams give an honest self-portrayal of the psyche's actual state. He says that "to me dreams are a part of nature, which harbors no intention to deceive, but expresses something as best it can, just as a plant grows or an animal seeks food as best it can" (1965, 161–162). Dreams appear strange not because of the trickery of a deceitful censor but because our conscious minds do not always understand the special symbolic language of the unconscious. If we want to discover what dreams mean, Jung argues, we must learn to speak their distinctive language of image, symbol, and metaphor.

Compensatory and Prospective Functions

Among the many functions that dreams serve (and he acknowledges that there are a number of different ones), there are two that Jung considers especially important. The first relates to the central process of *compensation*, which Jung believes governs the relationship between consciousness and the unconscious. Whereas Freud puts great emphasis on the development of rational consciousness, Jung argues that psychological health and development involve a progressive balancing of consciousness with the unconscious, with the more "irrational" aspects of the psyche. "We can take the theory of compensation as a basic law of psychic behavior," he says (1974, 101). Dreams are a powerful means of promoting the overall balance of the psyche because they bring forth unconscious contents that the conscious ego has either ignored, not valued sufficiently, or actively repressed.

In *Memories, Dreams, Reflections* Jung gives a personal example of a compensatory dream. He had realized, during an analysis with a female patient, that his dialogue with her was becoming increasingly shallow. Something was wrong, but he didn't know what it could be. So he decided to raise the issue with her in their next session. The night before that session, Jung had a dream: he is walking down a valley, with a steep hill on his right. On the top of the hill is a castle, and on the highest tower he sees a woman; in order to see her, he has to bend his head far back. At this point Jung woke up from the dream with a painful crick in the back of his neck. He immediately recognized the woman as his patient and thus realized what the dream meant: "If in the dream I had to look up at the patient in this fashion, in reality I had probably been looking down on her. Dreams are, after all, compensations for the conscious attitude." When Jung told his patient of the dream and his interpretation, he found that it produced an immediate and positive change in the therapeutic relationship (1965, 133).

The second valuable function of dreams, according to Jung, is to provide *prospective* visions of the future. He agrees with Freud that dreams may look backward to past experiences, but he argues that dreams also look forward to anticipate the dreamer's future development. Jung did not mean that all dreams necessarily predict the future, only that dreams frequently suggest what might happen, what potentials and possibilities the dreamer's future might hold.

Jung himself experienced a number of dreams that he believed accurately foretold future occurrences both in his personal life and in society. For example, in the fall of 1913 he had an hour-long vision of an ocean of blood rushing over the Alps and drowning all of Western civilization. Then, in the spring of 1914, he had a series of dreams in which an Arctic cold wave descended upon Europe and froze it to ice; all living things were killed by the frost (Jung 1965, 176). Just a few months after these dreams, World War I broke out.

Methods of Interpretation

Jung says that an analyst must start the interpretation of any dream with an admission of ignorance and a willingness to find something new—the interpreter must be open to whatever the dream has to say. Jung recommends that the first step should be to examine, in as much detail as possible, the dream's context in the individual's waking life. (Ideally, the dreamer has provided a series of dreams, for this will provide a broader picture of the individual's unconscious world than can be gained from a single dream.) Then, Jung says the analyst should seek *amplifications* of the dream's images and themes. Unlike Freud's process of free association, which Jung believes leads the dreamer away from the dream, amplification involves circling around the dream's images again and again, in an effort to discover deeper elements of the dream's meanings. If a man dreamed about a tall tree, for instance, he might free associate about his garden, a nearby park, a childhood experience climbing a tree, and so forth. All of this is interesting, Jung says, but not necessarily relevant to the dream about tall tree. Jung would encourage the dreamer to describe in detail how the tree in the dream appeared, how it was shaped, what color its leaves were; he would ask the dreamer what trees are like in general, how they grow, what nourishes them and what threatens them; he would ask how the tall tree makes the dreamer feel, what emotions come up in the dream—each of these questions working to keep the dreamer focused directly on the dream itself and on the complex web of meanings expressed in the image of the tall tree.

To help the dreamer in this process of amplification, Jung will sometimes note the parallels between a particular dream image and similar images in world mythology. In this example of the dream of the tall tree, such parallels might include the Tree of Knowledge, which the Bible describes as standing in the Garden of Eden; the ever verdant ash tree, Yggdrasil, which Nordic mythology says is rooted at the center of the world; and the Tree of Life, which in the Jewish mystical tradition of Kabbalism represents the divine ordering of the cosmos. Jung would bring up these parallels not to define what the dream means, but to give the dreamer new perspectives on that particular image of the tall tree.

One important question Jung asks in interpreting a dream is whether the dream's images and symbols relate primarily to the *objective* level of meaning or to the *subjective* level. To take a new example, a dream of fighting with an angry woman might relate to an actual experience the dreamer had the previous day of arguing with an angry woman; Jung would call this an interpretation on the objective level. The same dream could also relate to an emotional conflict within the dreamer, a conflict with "angry woman" elements of the dreamer's own psyche; Jung would call this an interpretation on the subjective level. More often than not, Jung focuses his attention on the subjective aspects of a dream. He once compared dreams to a "theater in which the dreamer is himself the scene, the player, the prompter, the producer, the author, the public and the critic. . . . [The subjective approach] conceives all the figures in the dream as personified features of the dreamer's own personality" (1974, 52). So if the dream of fighting with the angry woman had taken place inside a bank with a crowd watching, Jung would suggest that every element in the dream—the angry woman, the bank, the crowd—represents some element within the dreamer's psyche. (Jung expands on this idea of dreams as an internal theatrical play by saying that each dream can be analyzed into four dramatic components: an opening scene, the development of a plot, the emergence of a conflict, and the resolution. However, Jung himself rarely used this four-part model in his actual dream interpretation practice.)

Another method that Jung uses in interpreting a dream is called *active imagination*. In this process Jung asks a patient to sit quietly and concentrate on re-imagining the dream in all its details. Gradually, the dream's images and characters and feeling tones come to life again, opening up new meanings and insights to the dreamer. The key to active imagination is allowing the unconscious free access to consciousness, thereby enabling the dream to continue its dramatic unfolding. Jung likens the process to "dreaming the dream onward."

The practice of dream interpretation should in Jung's view be a matter of "joint reflection," a "dialectical process" in which both the analyst and the dreamer participate. The only legitimate criterion for a valid interpretation is its therapeutic value: if the interpretation brings forth meanings that help the dreamer, it is a valid interpretation. Jung says in an article titled "The Aims of Psychotherapy,"

It ought not matter to me whether the result of my musings on the dream is scientifically verifiable or tenable, otherwise I am pursuing an ulterior—and therefore autoerotic—aim. I must content myself wholly with the fact that the result means something to the patient and sets his life in motion again. I may allow myself only one criterion for the result of my labors. Does it work? (1966, 42–43).

Symbols, Archetypes, and the Collective Unconscious

The interpretation of symbols is central to Jung's approach to dreams. On the one hand he says that there are no fixed meanings to any symbols—all dream symbols must be related to the dreamer's unique waking life situation. But on the other hand he believes that dreams regularly contain *archetypal* symbols, whose meanings are universal, transcending the dreamer's individual consciousness. Jung's interpretations of dreams leave the realm of the individual's associations entirely when he discerns the presence of such archetypal symbols.

Jung had a dream in 1909 that gave him what he says was his first clear perceptions of the universal, transpersonal realms of the psyche. It came while he was traveling with Freud, on a steamship bound for the United States. The two had been invited to Clark University to receive honorary degrees, and during the long voyage across the Atlantic they spent many hours interpreting each other's dreams. One night Jung had a dream in which he finds himself in the second story of a house, what he feels is *his* house. He goes downstairs, and when he reaches the ground floor he sees that all the furniture and decorations date from medieval times. He then follows a stone stairway down another floor to the cellar, which he discovers is a dwelling from ancient Rome. He sees a stone slab on the floor, opens it, and descends into a dark cave, strewn with bones and the remains of a primitive culture. On the dusty floor of the cave he sees two human skulls, very old and half disintegrated (1965, 157–161).

Jung shared this dream with Freud, who insisted that the two skulls must be expressing some powerful wish. Jung sensed that the wish Freud had in mind was a secret death wish; but Jung felt a "violent resistance" to such an interpretation (1965, 161). Instead, he saw the dream as a revelation of a "collective *a priori* beneath the personal psyche"—a realm of the unconscious that reaches far beyond the individual's personal life (1965, 161). For Jung the dream was a "structural diagram of the human psyche" showing that below the *personal unconscious* of our memories and experiences there is a *collective unconscious* which connects us at a fundamental level with the whole evolutionary history of humankind.

The claim that dreams express not just personal contents but also collective contents is one of the most distinctive features of Jung's dream theory. Archetypes, Jung explains, are universal psychic images that underlie and structure all human mental functioning. They are inherited patterns of thought which the human mind uses to frame perceptions, experiences, and feelings. Jung insists that archetypes are not themselves specific images, but are rather blueprints for images—with the actual content to be filled in with material from the individual's life. Archetypal symbols reflect a natural wisdom ingrained deeply within the human unconscious, and when they appear in dreams they can provide the dreamer with especially profound insights and guidance. Jung found that the world's religious and mythological traditions contain a wealth of archetypal images, symbols, and themes; and he recommended that anyone intending to practice dream interpretation should make a detailed study of these traditions.

Among the most common archetypes described by Jung in his writings are the persona, the shadow, the anima and animus, and the Self.

The *persona* archetype represents the basic human need to present ourselves favorably in society. Jung frequently likens the persona to a mask we put on when we appear in public—the persona is necessary both to protect vulnerable aspects of the individual's personality and to promote the smooth, efficient functioning of community life. A dream of behaving inappropriately in a social situation might indicate that the dreamer's persona is weak, that the mask is in danger of falling off. A dream of being trapped in a party or a group of people might indicate that the mask has become too tightly attached, that the dreamer cannot separate social appearances from his or her own true identity.

The *shadow* archetype represents all those unconscious elements and energies of the psyche that are poorly integrated with the individual's consciousness—these elements may be separated from consciousness, but they are still connected to it, and follow the individual around "like a shadow." Jung characterized the shadow as a dark other within us, as the primitive, instinctual aspects of ourselves which challenge the dominance of light, civilization, and consciousness. However, the shadow may in some cases express the brighter or more positive aspects of an individual's personality; for example, a violent criminal who has overly actualized the psyche's aggressive energies may have dreams filled with shadow images of kindness, nurturance, and altruism. Whether dark or light, the shadow archetype regularly appears in nightmares, particularly nightmares in which the dreamer is being chased by a frightening animal, monster, or vengeful murderer. Such terrifying dreams reveal that the dreamer's conscious attitude is in conflict with the shadow elements of his or her unconscious. The dreamer's task is then to confront those elements, understand them, and try to integrate them with consciousness.

The *anima* archetype represents the female aspects of a man's psyche, and the *animus* archetype represents the male aspects of a woman's psyche. All people, Jung believes, carry within them biological and psychological elements of the opposite sex. The anima and animus archetypes express the relationship of those elements to the individual's conscious personality. Our parents provide the original material out of which anima and animus images are formed; social stereotypes about the proper gender roles of men and women provide further material. The anima and animus appear in dreams to help people create psychological balance between the feminine and masculine energies within them. Jung says that these archetypes can also represent "soul-images," serving as potential mediators or guides in the individual's efforts to integrate consciousness and the unconscious.

The archetype of the *Self* represents the human potential to achieve wholeness and self-realization, to unite all the psychological opposites into a harmonious totality. Although such complete wholeness is rarely achieved, Jung says the archetype of the Self exists to remind us that it is a genuine potential within our psyche. Images of the Self are frequently expressed, both in dreams and in religious traditions, by *mandalas*. Mandalas are pictorial designs with intricately symmetrical patterns surrounding an accentuated center. Many mandalas take the form of flowers, crosses, and wheels. The number four, Jung finds, is a universally recurrent element in their design. When mandala imagery appears in a dream it generally addresses the dreamer's current relationship to his or her own potential for psychological wholeness. A dream of four trees, in which three of the trees are tall and healthy while the fourth is short and sickly, might suggest that one element of the dreamer's potential psychic wholeness needs to be given greater attention and nurturance.

JUNG'S VIEWS ON INDIVIDUATION, RELIGION, AND MODERN SOCIETY

Mandala imagery in dreams reveals what Jung believes is the ultimate nature and function of dreaming: dreams promote the basic evolutionary process of bringing consciousness and the unconscious into balance, wholeness, and integration—the process Jung calls *individuation*. Individuation is the "complete actualization of the whole human being" (1974, 108). It represents, Jung believes, the true and final goal of all life. A common misunderstanding of this central concept in Jung's psychology is that individuation means rejecting consciousness and giving free rein to the unconscious. Jung repeatedly emphasizes that consciousness has the vital task of understanding and actualizing the contents that rise up from the unconscious—neither controlling nor surrendering to them but integrating them into a broader, more balanced conscious self-awareness. "In the final analysis," Jung says, "the decisive factor is always consciousness, which can understand the manifestations of the unconscious and take up a position towards them" (1965, 187).

As dream experiences demonstrate, the individuation process unfolds naturally within the life of each human being. Throughout history this process has been encouraged, guided, and nurtured by the world's religious and mythological traditions. Jung believes that religions have always served to promote the union of consciousness and the unconscious. The individuation process is at the core of all sacred teachings, from the mythic lore of Australian Aborigines and Native Americans to the grand theological systems of Christians and Buddhists. Jung devotes many of his writings to detailed analyses of the archetypal symbolism to be found in world religions. He gives special attention to Gnosticism, a first-century A.D. merging of Greek mysticism with early Christianity, and Alchemy, a medieval tradition of natural philosophy. Jung argues that the Gnostics and Alchemists already knew what modern psychologists are just now discovering about the deepest realms of the unconscious.

Jung believes that traditional religious beliefs, symbols, and rites no longer function effectively for many people in modern Western society. The rise of rational science, the growing power of technology, and the ever-increasing complexity and hurriedness of modern life have all combined to tear people away from their roots in religious and mythological traditions. As a result, increasing numbers of people are suffering from dangerous psychological imbalances. The more humans have developed their powers of reason, the more they have ignored or repressed the "irrational" elements within their psyches. Jung says that the twentieth century's bloody history of violence and warfare proves that our great advances in civilization have in fact provoked these destructive outbursts of primitive aggression.

The goal of modern psychotherapy, in Jung's view, is to perform the services that religious traditions used to perform: helping people find their own balanced wholeness, their own path toward individuation. Dreams are an invaluable resource in psychotherapy because they show both the present condition of the dreamer's psychological development and the dreamer's future possibilities of growing toward greater self-integration. In one of his case studies Jung makes a lengthy analysis of a patient's dreams, examining the many parallels between the dream series and images from ancient myths, spiritual traditions, and mystical teachings. The case demonstrates that modern individuals, no matter how rational, civilized, and secular they have become, will still find in their unconscious essentially religious yearnings toward personal wholeness. Jung says this case "proves that even if the conscious mind is miles away from the ancient conceptions of the rites of renewal, the unconscious still strives to bring them closer in dreams" (1974, 211).

Indeed, Jung believes that it is precisely because modern people have an overly rational worldview that religious compensations emerge in our dreams, working to balance that one-sided conscious outlook. While religious compensations through what Jung calls "*big dreams*" are rare, their power and influence can be tremendous: "'big' dreams . . . are often remembered for a lifetime, and not infrequently prove to be the richest jewel in the treasure-house of psychic experience" (1974, 36). However, Jung repeatedly warns that people should not underestimate the real dangers that face anyone who truly descends into the depths of the unconscious. Jung tells the story of an apparently normal man who came to Zurich wanting to be trained as an analyst. After several weeks of failing to remember any dreams at all, the man finally had a dream which he shared with Jung. In the dream the man takes a train to a city; he wanders through the streets and comes to an area filled with medieval buildings; he goes inside one, gets dreadfully lost, and finally stumbles into a large, dark room—and in the middle of the room he finds an idiot child, about two years old, smeared with its own feces. The man told Jung he awoke from this dream in a panic. When Jung heard the dream, he immediately recognized it as an indication of a latent psychosis: the man was in grave danger of losing conscious control to the terribly primitive, childlike forces within him. Jung politely but firmly discouraged the man from further analytic training. This case, Jung says, shows that people should be very careful when stirring up the unconscious. With this man, "his emphatic normality reflected a personality which would not have been developed but simply shattered by a confrontation with the unconscious" (1965, 136).

JUNG'S ANSWERS TO THE THREE BASIC QUESTIONS

Formation

Dreams are formed out of material from the personal unconscious (e.g., thoughts, feelings, and experiences from daily life) and from the collective unconscious (e.g., the archetypes of the persona, shadow, anima and animus, self). The rich imagery and complex symbolism of dreams is simply the natural means by which the unconscious expresses itself. Dreams do not intentionally hide their meanings but rather express them honestly and directly, in the best way they can. Jung believes that the ultimate power behind the formation of dreams comes from a transpersonal realm far beyond the individual's own psyche.

Function

The major function of dreams is to compensate for the imbalances of the conscious personality. Dreams bring forth unconscious elements of the psyche which the individual has ignored or repressed; dreams challenge the individual to integrate those elements with consciousness and thus develop a deeper, more balanced self-awareness. A second important function of dreams is to provide prospective visions of future potentials and possibilities in the dreamer's life. Overall, the function of dreams is to promote the basic psychological process of individuation, the individual's natural yearning to grow toward ever greater wholeness and self-actualization.

Interpretation

As a regular, natural process dreams do not need to be consciously interpreted and understood in order to fulfill their functions. However, Jung believes that these functions can be greatly enhanced by the practice of dream interpretation. Jung's method is first to clarify the dream's context in the waking life situation of the dreamer and then to seek amplifications of the dream's imagery: carefully circling around the dream, gradually discovering the complex web of meanings and emotions expressed by each particular image. The practice of amplification frequently draws on the world's religious and mythological traditions to provide further insights into the dream's meanings. Jung looks at how the dream may relate to the dreamer's experiences in the "objective" reality of external society, and also how the dream's characters, settings, and events may represent "subjective" aspects of the individual's inner world. The conscious interpretation of dreams has tremendous value for psychotherapy because it powerfully stimulates the process of individuation. Especially for modern Westerners, dream interpretation can be a potent means of reconnecting their rational, conscious selves with the essentially religious elements of their psychic depths.

NOTES

1. Virtually every biography of Jung argues that there are good reasons to be skeptical about the accuracy and sufficiency of what Jung reveals of himself in *Memories, Dreams, Reflections*. Most strikingly, Jung says almost nothing in the book about the personal relationships in his life. He speaks in some detail of his parents and of Freud, but of very few others.

2. During this time Jung also had a very intimate relationship with Toni Wolff, one of his patients (Jung never mentions her in *Memories, Dreams, Reflections*). Many biographers have suggested that Jung's relationship with her was crucial in helping him through these years of inner crisis, and that there are parallels here with Freud's relationship with Fliess. See Homans 1979, 75-76.

3. In the evaluation of Jung's life, it is important to note that this inner crisis of 1912-1918 coincided almost exactly with World War I (1914-1918).

Chapter 4

Alternative Clinical Theories About Dreams

> Goebbels was visiting my factory. He had all the workers line up in two rows facing each other. I had to stand in the middle and raise my arm in the Nazi salute. It took me half an hour to get my arm up, inch by inch. Goebbels showed neither approval nor disapproval as he watched my struggle, as if it were a play. When I finally managed to get my arm up, he said just five words—'I don't want your salute'—then turned and went to the door. There I stood in my own factory, arm raised, pilloried right in the midst of my own people. I was only able to keep from collapsing by staring at his clubfoot as he limped out. And so I stood until I woke up.
>
> Sixty-year old German factory owner, 1936, in Beradt 1966, 5

A Freudian interpretation of this dream would seek personal associations to each of the dream's parts and trace the associations back to repressed unconscious wishes. The image of Joseph Goebbels, the notorious Nazi Minister of Culture, would likely be interpreted as a father figure, with the slow, painful raising of the arm symbolizing the dreamer's feelings of impotence and oedipal anxiety. A Jungian interpretation, by contrast, would try to amplify the dream's elements, and it would look to see if the unconscious is compensating for imbalances in the dreamer's conscious attitudes. The humiliation that the factory owner suffers in the dream might be an unconscious corrective to an excessive pride and arrogance in his waking life, and the evil Goebbels might be a shadow figure representing the violent, totalitarian forces in his own psyche.

Are these the only two ways of approaching a dream? Many people have assumed that Freud and Jung simply *are* the psychology of dreaming: there is Freud's theory, there is Jung's theory, and then there are minor commentaries on them. In one sense this assumption is valid. No one has written a book to rival Freud's *Interpretation of Dreams*, and no one has probed the universe of dream symbolism as deeply as Jung. However, the theories of Freud and Jung do not exhaustively answer all important questions about dreaming. A number of psychologists have learned from Freud and Jung and then gone on to develop alternative approaches to dreaming, approaches based on different theoretical frameworks and different clinical practices.

This chapter will describe four major clinical theories about dreams that arose after Freud and Jung: the Individual Psychology of Alfred Adler, the Existential Psychoanalysis of Medard Boss, the Ego Psychology of Thomas French and Erika Fromm, and the Gestalt Psychology of Frederick Perls. These are by no means the only alternatives to Freud and Jung, but they are certainly among the most innovative and influential of those alternative dream theories.[1]

INDIVIDUAL PSYCHOLOGY: ALFRED ADLER

Alfred Adler was a Viennese doctor who became one of the earliest members of Freud's psychoanalytic circle. From 1902 to 1911 he wrote several papers on Freudian theory and participated actively in the newly founded Viennese Psychoanalytic Society. In 1910 he was elected to be the group's president. But eventually Adler and Freud realized that their views diverged on many key theoretical issues. In 1911 Adler resigned from the Society and formed his own organization, which he called the Society for Individual Psychology. He wrote and taught extensively throughout the rest of his career and had a large (but often unacknowledged) influence on many later schools of psychology.[2]

Adler's approach to dreams starts with the basic assertion that all humans have an innate drive to preserve the unity of their personalities: "the supreme law of both life-forms, sleep and wakefulness alike, is this: the sense of worth of the self shall not be allowed to be diminished" (1956, 358). Adler refers to this innate, dynamic drive as a striving to achieve *superiority* (in the sense of freedom, security, power) and, conversely, to overcome *inferiority*. Adler says he sees

in every psychological phenomenon the striving for superiority. It runs parallel to physical growth and is an intrinsic necessity of life itself. It lies at the root of all solutions of life's problems and is manifested in the way in which we meet these problems. All our functions follow its direction. . . . The urge from below to above never ceases. Whatever premises all our philosophers and psychologists dream of—self-preservation, pleasure principle, equalization—all these are but vague representations, attempts to express the great upward drive. (103)

The various behaviors that each person uses to defend this sense of superiority and self-worth make up what Adler calls "the individual's style of life" (358).

In sharp contrast to Freud and Jung, Adler argues that consciousness and the unconscious are not opposed to each other; they are fundamentally united, in that both express the individual's style of life. Adler therefore concentrates exclusively on how dreams relate to the individual's day-to-day existence, rather than using dreams to delve into the deep unconscious realms of the psyche. At the most basic level, then, Adler considers dreams valuable because they are a diagnostic tool that psychotherapists can use to learn about the characteristic pattern of behaviors, beliefs, and attitudes that a patient uses to preserve his or her personal integrity and style of life.

To interpret dreams Adler relies first on the free association method of Freud, eliciting from the dreamer whatever thoughts and memories arise in connection with the dream. Adler also follows Freud in looking very carefully at the emotional content of a dream, because he believes that the emotions a person feels in a dream reveal key elements of his or her particular style of life. But Adler departs from Freud on the issue of universal symbols; he says that "we must modify each dream interpretation to fit the individual concerned; and each individual is different. . . . The only valid dream interpretation is that which can be integrated with an individual's general behavior, early memories, [and] problems" (363).

Adler grants that dreams serve a kind of problem-solving function, but in his view this function is deceptive and ultimately ineffectual. When a person faces a problem in life that challenges the resources of his or her style of life, a dream will respond by metaphorically reworking the problem until it can be solved using the person's ordinary coping strategies. For instance, a man who was dissatisfied with his family life might have a dream in which he criticizes his wife for failing to take care of their children. In Adler's view such a dream would have taken a life problem the man had been unable to solve (his general unhappiness with family life) and transformed it into a more limited problem which he *could* solve (his wife being an incompetent mother). Adler says, "in dreams we fool ourselves into an inadequate solution of a problem, that is, inadequate from the standpoint of common sense, but adequate from the standpoint of our style of life" (360). Dreams are essentially self-protective fantasies that reduce our problems to a size we feel we can manage.

So for Adler, dreaming is a function of failed adaptation to waking reality. Dreams occur when there is a conflict between a person's style of life and the demands of "reality and common sense"; they are "self-deceptions" that try desperately to preserve the person's sense of unity and self-worth (360). But because the aim of Individual Psychology is to increase an individual's courage to meet the problems of life, Adler's basic approach to dreams is to use them as illustrations of where the person is weakest and in most need of developing greater rational judgment. Indeed, Adler suggested that people who deal adequately with their problems "in the daytime" do not need to dream at all: "We should expect, therefore, that the more the individual goal agrees with reality the less a person dreams; and we find that it is so. Very courageous people dream rarely, for they deal adequately with their situation in the daytime" (360). One commentator has noted that Adler seems to have dreamed very little himself, remarking "it sounds very much as if Adler adapted his theory to accommodate the fact that at some point he personally stopped remembering his dreams" (Shafton 1995, 138).

EXISTENTIAL PSYCHOANALYSIS: MEDARD BOSS

Medard Boss was a Swiss psychoanalyst who, following his training in Freudian clinical practice, worked for ten years with Jung in Zurich. But, as he says in the preface to his major work *The Analysis of Dreams*, he gradually realized that Freud, Jung, and all the other leading dream psychologists were making the same faulty assumption: "[T]hey replaced the immediate and direct phenomenon by explanations of it. They saw in dreams the expression of something else, something merely assumed to exist behind the phenomena, some mental construct" (1958, 9). Boss decided that what was needed was greater attention to "the dream phenomenon itself," apart from all theories and hypotheses and clinical models. He became very interested in the work of Ludwig Binswanger, who as founder of the *Daseinanalyse* or existentialist approach to psychology had been working to integrate Freudian psychoanalysis with the thought of German philosopher Martin Heidegger. After making his own careful study of Heidegger's work, and particularly Heidegger's central concept of "being-in-the-world" (*Dasein*), Boss developed his own distinctive existentialist approach to dreams.

Boss, like Adler, rejects the idea that consciousness and the unconscious are two radically different, mutually opposed aspects of the psyche. But unlike Adler, Boss uses a sophisticated philosophical framework to support and develop his position. For Boss the unity of conscious and unconscious life is based on the primary ontological fact that we always exist in relationship with things and people; these relationships *are* what we are. Humans do not possess any essence or nature that can be identified outside of our relationships, outside of our "being-in-the-world." Boss further argues that this basic philosophical truth applies to all our experiences: waking life and dreaming life are but different modes of our existential relatedness to the world.

Boss draws three important implications regarding dreams from existentialist philosophy. The first is that dreams are real experiences, real in the sense of expressing a genuine mode of being-in-the-world. For this reason Boss believes that dreams deserve no less attention and respect than we give to our waking life experiences. The second implication is that when we try to understand dreams we must set aside all our assumptions and look at the dreams themselves, exactly as they present themselves to us. Boss rejects Freud's manifest-latent content distinction and, likewise, Jung's method of amplification; in both cases, he says, the dream experience itself is obscured by the interpreter's theoretical biases and expectations. What Boss calls for is an exclusive focus on what the dreamer does, feels, and experiences in the dream, in the particular mode of being-in-the-world he or she experiences while dreaming.

The third implication regards the question of dream symbolism. Boss argues that dreams do not "symbolize" anything, but rather involve real, tangible experiences.

For instance, he would see a vivid dream of flying as a genuine actualization of the dreamer's innate human possibility for freedom. Boss believes that talking about what such a dream symbolizes (e.g., sexuality, ego inflation, etc.) only leads the dreamer away from the concrete experience felt within the dream.

In *The Analysis of Dreams* Boss recounts the story of one of his patients, an engineer in his forties, who came to Boss for psychotherapy because of depression and sexual impotence. The engineer told Boss he had never dreamed once in his entire life—until just two days before their first analytic session. In this dream the engineer is imprisoned in a dungeon whose bars are made of mathematical signs and numbers. After the analysis got started, the engineer began bringing new dreams to every session. Boss noticed that during the first six and a half months the engineer dreamed only of machines, cars, planes, and electrical devices. Then, for the first time, he dreamed of a living thing—a potted plant. Four months later the engineer began dreaming of insects, all of them dangerous and harmful. After that he dreamed for a time of toads, frogs, and snakes. The first mammal to appear in the engineer's dreams was a mouse, which scurried down a mouse hole the instant it was seen. Next were dreams of pigs, then of lions and horses. After two years of analysis the engineer finally dreamed of a human being. In that dream he discovered a giant unconscious woman, in a long blood-red dress, trapped under an ice-covered pond; terrified, he ran for help. Six months later, the engineer dreamed that he was dancing at a party with a vibrant woman dressed in a similar blood-red outfit and that they fell in passionate love with each other.

Boss reports that the engineer's depression had begun disappearing by the time of the potted plant dream, and his sexual potency had returned when he began dreaming of lions and horses. The engineer's dreams revealed that his depression and impotence were ultimately caused by his being a prisoner of "his life-denying mathematical thought. . . . In these dreams he [the engineer] became aware of his imprisonment with a clarity which far surpassed that of waking life" (115). Boss says that existential psychotherapy helped the engineer escape from his bondage to abstract technical thought. The engineer's long dream series (823 dreams in all) showed the gradual flowering of "his full human potentiality" (115).

Boss believes that dreams both mirror our present being-in-the-world and also open us to future potentials and possibilities. He describes the dream of a very promiscuous businessman who, though raised a Protestant, was a cynical atheist in adulthood. In his dream the businessman goes to a monastery built high above a river and talks with a "high Catholic priest" about buying the monastery. The priest can't speak for long, though, because he has to go say mass. As the priest goes the businessman suddenly notices his robes, which are "glowing with indescribable beauty" (144). Boss says that while this man's waking existence had been dominated by "the animality of sexual behavior," his dreaming existence was able to perceive with great clarity the existence of "higher regions": "new possibilities of being have opened up to him. Into the dream world of this atheist there is suddenly admitted a high Catholic priest. With the appearance of this priest a door to the religious sphere is opened for the dreamer" (144).

Transformative experiences of new possibility come forth in dreams because of the tremendous freedom we have in our dreaming mode of being-in-the-world. This is why dreams are so valuable in psychotherapy, because they point to those places in people's lives where they are most constricted, and help people discover their innate existential capacity for free choice and action. And beyond this practical usefulness in psychotherapy, dreams disclose people's most sublime and transcendental potentials for growth. Boss says we should pay special attention to extremely unusual dream phenomena, for these experiences bring forth radically new possibilities of being-in-the-world. Extrasensory dreams that predict future illnesses and accidents, dreams within dreams that challenge the nature of personal identity, ecstatic dreams that bring people into contact with the Divine—while some psychologists argue that such dreams are impossible, Boss insists that it is precisely in extraordinary dream experiences like these that we most fully recognize and actualize our true existential freedom.

EGO PSYCHOLOGY: THOMAS FRENCH AND ERICH FROMM

Ego Psychology is a branch of psychoanalysis that draws its inspiration from Freud's later writings about the ego's capacity to master both internal and external realities. Analysts like Anna Freud (Freud's youngest daughter), Heinz Hartmann, and Erik Erikson developed Freud's ideas into a new psychotherapeutic approach that put special emphasis on strengthening the patient's ego—helping it defend against anxiety, control unruly instinctual impulses, and adapt more successfully to the demands of social reality. Although Erikson wrote an excellent paper in which he offers a new interpretation of Freud's "Dream of Irma's Injection," the most influential work on dreams from the Ego Psychology perspective has been done by Thomas French and Erich Fromm. Both were classically-trained psychoanalysts, and they collaborated on a number of articles about dreams and on the book *Dream Interpretation: A New Approach* (1964).

French and Fromm do not dispute Freud's original dream theory so much as reorient it, pointing it toward the practical waking-life situation of the dreamer's ego. They view every dream as an attempt by the ego to solve a current life problem, which appears as the focal conflict of the dream. For example, a male patient who was married and the father of three children reported dreaming that he "was mixing cement." While free associating to the dream he mentioned that his house needed some repair work done on its external walls. French and Fromm say that this very brief dream expresses an effort to solve a key emotional problem in the man's life—how to take better care of his family, how to "hold their house together." However, the dream shows that the strategy he is using to solve this problem is inadequate; "instead of interacting with his wife and children directly, he 'mixes (lifeless) cement'" (1992, 185).

As this example indicates, dreams reveal not only what the focal conflict is, but how the dreamer is trying to solve it. French and Fromm believe that dreams have great value as illustrations of a person's basic cognitive structure, his or her ego's favorite defensive and integrative strategies to use in dealing with waking life problems.

In the case of longer and more elaborate dreams, the focal conflict is brought into relation with analogous conflicts and problems that the dreamer has faced in the past. A person who is having troubles with a supervisor at work might dream of past conflicts with authorities, like parents, priests, teachers, and so on; the dream would bring up these memories in order to help the ego see what worked, and what didn't work, when the person came up against similar problems earlier in life. These elements and memories from the past constitute the dream's historical background, and French and Fromm insist that a better understanding of this historical background can provide valuable assistance in the dreamer's efforts to solve the focal conflict.

People often wonder why dreams portray such a hodgepodge of characters and settings—a dream might take us back to our third-grade classroom, but have decorations and furniture like a hotel from some long-ago vacation, and yet be filled with people whom we saw yesterday at a grocery store. What possible meaning could all this have? French and Fromm argue that the seemingly garbled content of people's dreams *always* has a meaning: dreams will bring up anything, any memory, image, or experience, that might be relevant to the ego's need to solve the current focal conflict. Stated differently, this means that every element in the dream, no matter how random or bizarre, is connected to the focal conflict.

This makes interpreting dreams difficult, French and Fromm admit, because the same dream may show the focal conflict being denied, being addressed in a childish fashion, being compared to other current life problems, and being maturely and creatively resolved, all at the same time. Thus, they recommend that interpreters try to use a variety of approaches and, most importantly, to rely on their empathetic imaginations to guide them. French and Fromm compare interpreting a dream to interpreting a work of art, in that the first step of the process should be allowing one's intuition and imagination to scan the dream. By listening carefully for little hints of significance, and by moving back and forth between the dream as a whole and its various parts, the analyst will gradually formulate an interpretive hypothesis about the dream's overall meaning. French and Fromm explain that "the interpretive hypothesis is correct if it illuminates or explains every bit of the dream text plus every single association given to it as parts of a *total response the dreamer has made to his actual current emotional situation*" (194). Failure in dream interpretation comes from unwillingness to follow one's intuitions, from getting "side-tracked on a Sub-Focal Conflict," and from becoming prematurely tied to one hypothesis about the dream's meaning. There are two tests to use in judging an interpretive hypothesis: the scientific one of critically checking the dream and associations for any inconsistencies with the hypothesis, and the aesthetic one of feeling pleasure at the beautiful whole of the dream, a sense of recognizing the dream in its totality, "usually with a joyful 'Aha'" experience (188).

Ultimately, French and Fromm believe that the goals of dream interpretation are to identify the focal conflict, to clarify the cognitive structure the dreamer is using to solve that conflict, and thereby to facilitate better waking-life functioning.

GESTALT PSYCHOLOGY: FREDERICK PERLS

Frederick Perls was a German medical doctor who combined Freudian psycho-analysis, existentialism, and Gestalt psychology into an innovative and highly influential approach to dream therapy. Perls did his basic psychoanalytic training in Germany, but when the Nazis came to power in the 1930s he left the country and emigrated to South Africa. While working there he studied the growing body of psychological research on the Gestalt aspects of cognitive functioning. ("Gestalt" is a German word meaning form, pattern, shape.) This research suggested that human perception is a matter of instantly grasping complexly interrelated patterns. We don't initially perceive two legs, two arms, curly hair, freckles, a big smile, and then conclude "That's my friend Tom"; rather, we initially perceive the total *Gestalt* of Tom, the overall pattern which can later be broken down into separate perceptual elements like legs, hair, smile, and so forth. Perls expanded Gestalt psychology's concepts to psychotherapeutic practice, helping people learn to recognize and expand the Gestalt of their own individual personalities. He agreed with leaders of the Humanistic Psychology movement like Abraham Maslow and Carl Rogers that psychoanalytic and behaviorist models of psychology only speak about the absence of pain and unhappiness—they say nothing positive about what a healthy, fulfilling life is like. In his writings and especially in his therapy groups (conducted most famously at the Esalen Institute in Big Sur, California, in the mid-1960s), Perls developed an approach to dreams which aimed to promote not just the cure of neurosis but the experience of creative, healthy living.

Perls says that "all impoverishment of the personality comes about by self-alienation—by disowning parts of ourselves" (1970b, 212). All psychological illness is caused by holes in the Gestalt of an individual's personality. To cure illness and to enhance genuine health, the disowned parts must be reclaimed and reintegrated into the personality Gestalt. Dreams are in Perls's view one of the very best means of learning where the holes in an individual's personality lie. "Freud once called the dream 'the royal road to the unconscious,'" Perls says, "[but] I believe that it is really the royal road to *integration*" (1970b, 204).[3]

Perls regards dreams as spontaneous creations of the dreamer himself or herself. As such, every element of a dream reflects some element of the dreamer. Nothing in a dream is coincidental, nothing is meaningless. Every aspect of a dream "is a part of the dreamer, but a part that to some extent is disowned and projected onto other objects" (Perls 1970a, 27). Although this sounds similar to Jung's notion of the subjective level of interpretation (see Chapter 3), Perls is actually making a quite different claim about the nature of dreaming. He does not speak of dreams as tapping into deep archetypal undercurrents flowing in and through each individual psyche; rather, Perls considers dreaming as the direct product of the individual self, "an existential message . . . of yourself to yourself" (1970a, 27).

The therapeutic approach Perls takes toward dreams is guided by the basic existential principle of trying to help the dreamer re-experience the dream in the waking state as immediately, as intensely, and as fully as possible. Because each element in the dream reflects some disowned part of the individual's personality, the individual can begin to reintegrate those parts by identifying with each of the dream's parts. Perls disdains any kind of dream analysis that distracts the dreamer from the feelings and sensations experienced in the dream. He insists that people describe their dreams in the present tense, not the past, and encourages them to imagine *being* each element of a given dream. Below is a sample dialogue from one of Perls's dream seminars. A woman ("C.") has described a dream in which she sees a lake that is drying up, with some porpoises on an island, and an old license plate on the bottom of the lake:

Perls: *Will you please play this license plate.*
  C.:   I am an old license plate, thrown in the bottom of a lake. I have no use because I'm of no value. I'm not rusted, I'm outdated. So, I can't be used. I'm just thrown on the rubbish heap. That's what I did with the license plate—I threw it in the rubbish heap.
Perls: *Well, what do you feel about the dream?*
  C.:   I don't like it. I don't like being an old license plate—useless.
Perls: *Could you talk about it until you come to be the license plate.*
  C.:   Useless—outdated. The use of the license plate is to allow—to give a car permission to go—and I can't give anyone permission to do anything because I'm outdated. In California they just paste a little—you buy a sticker and stick it on the car—on the old license plates. So, maybe someone would put me on their car and stick a new sticker on me. I don't . . .
Perls: *O.K. Play now the lake.*
  C.:   I am a lake. I am drying up and disappearing—soaking into the earth—*dying*. But, when I soak into the earth and become part of the earth maybe, I water the surrounding area, so—even the lake—even in my bed—flowers can grow. New, like can grow from me—[C. is starting to cry]
Perls: *Do you get the existential message?*
  C.:   Yes, I can—I can create. I can create beauty. . . . [As] the water and the lake, I can play a part. (1970b, 213–214)

As this dialogue indicates, Perls encourages his clients to identify with or play the role of every element in their dreams: feeling what it's like to *be* that element, looking at the rest of the dream from its special perspective, and reflecting on how that element has been expressed, or disowned, in the Gestalt of the dreamer's personality.

Perls also guides his clients in exploring areas of tension between elements in the dream that oppose or conflict with each other. He gives particular attention to instances of what he calls the "topdog vs. underdog" opposition. "Topdog" is the demanding voice of our ideals, trying to control our behavior, forcing us to be good; "underdog" is the unsteady voice of our resentments, unable to fight topdog directly but determined to resist its righteous demands. Perls believes that many dreams express topdog vs. underdog "games" within the dreamer's personality. For example, if a man dreamed of an adult angrily trying to punish a disobedient child, Perls would have the dreamer identify first with the adult, then with the child, then back and forth, letting the two opposing dream characters dialogue and really "have it out." In this way the dreamer would be able to experience both the topdog adult and the underdog child as aspects of himself. Perls would try to help the dreamer move from having a conflict between the adult and child to *being both*, and thus to integrating them.

While admitting that this process is not easy, Perls says "if we work long enough, then you come through to an understanding and . . . an appreciation of differences" (1970b, 212). Successful Gestalt dream therapy enables people to stop projecting disowned parts of themselves out onto the world, and to begin taking full responsibility for all aspects of their personality. With a total acceptance of one's actual self and a commitment to living in the "here and now," Perls believes that people will finally be able to "*wake up* and become real. . . . The task of *all* deep religions, especially Zen Buddhism, or of good therapy, is the Great Awakening—the coming *to one's senses*—waking up from one's dream, especially from one's nightmare" (1970b, 215).

ALTERNATIVE CLINICAL ANSWERS TO THE THREE BASIC QUESTIONS

Formation

On the question of how dreams are formed, the four theories discussed in this chapter all see a fundamental continuity between the nature of dreaming and waking experience. Adler, Boss, and Perls all reject the notion (shared by Freud and Jung) that dreams originate far away in the depths of the unconscious; they insist that dreams are shaped by the same personality structures that operate while we're awake—Adler's "style of life," Boss's "being-in-the-world," Perls's "spontaneous creativity." French and Fromm, while retaining many elements of Freud's dream theory, also put greater emphasis on the connection of dreaming and waking patterns of personality (what they call a dream's "cognitive structure").

Function

Adler is alone among the four in minimizing the positive, constructive, creative functions of dreaming. Like Freud, he sees dreams as self-deceptions that are useful only in diagnosing weaknesses and failings in the personality. Boss, French and Fromm, and Perls also believe that dreams provide valuable diagnostic insights into the dreamer's current psychological condition, but they go on to argue that dreams can bring forth new creative energies that lead beyond the ordinary capacities of the dreamer's waking consciousness. Perls calls dreams "the royal road to integration" for their capacity to help people reclaim parts of themselves that they have disowned. French and Fromm see dreams as elaborate and often very creative efforts to solve a focal problem in the dreamer's life. Boss says that the extraordinary freedom people experience while dreaming enables the discovery of truly transcendental aspects of human existence.

Interpretation

All four theories speak out against rigid, formulaic methods of dream interpretation, and they insist that any interpretation must be grounded in the realities of the dreamer's personal life. Adler's approach puts special emphasis on the emotions felt during a dream, taking them as significant clues to discovering the dreamer's style of life. French and Fromm regard dream interpretation as akin to the interpretation of art, in the need to follow the guidance of one's intuition and empathetic imagination. The theories of both Adler and French and Fromm are close to Freud's in relying heavily on the dreamer's free associations and in seeking a comprehensive explanation of every detail of a given dream. Boss and Perls, however, depart sharply from Freud. Boss dismisses free association, amplification, and anything else that leads the dreamer away from the immediate felt experience of the dream; he asks not what a dream symbolizes, but what mode of being-in-the-world the dreamer experiences in the dream. Similarly, Perls rejects the overly intellectual cast of Freudian interpretation and encourages the dreamer to identify with each element of the dream, as an element of the dreamer's own self.

NOTES

1. By many accounts the best introductory textbook regarding the practical application of dreams in clinical psychotherapeutic contexts is Walter Bonime's *The Clinical Use of Dreams* (1988).

2. "It would not be easy to find another author from which so much has been borrowed from all sides without acknowledgment than Alfred Adler" (Ellenberger 1970, 645).

3. Recall that the exact wording from *The Interpretation of Dreams* is somewhat different: "The interpretation of dreams is the royal road to a knowledge of the unconscious activities of the mind" (Freud 1965a, 647).

Chapter 5

Sleep Laboratories, REM Sleep, and Dreaming

I had been dreaming about getting ready to take some kind of exam. It had been a very short dream. That's just about all that it contained. I don't think I was worried about it.

I was dreaming about exams. In the early part of the dream, I was dreaming that I had just finished taking an exam and it was a very sunny day outside. I was walking with a boy who was in some of my classes with me. There was a sort of a . . . a break, and someone mentioned a grade they had gotten in a social science exam, and I asked them if the social science marks had come in. They said yes. I didn't get mine because I had been away for a day.

> Two dreams, the first from NREM sleep and the second from REM sleep, reported by the same subject on the same night, from Dement, 1972, 44

In the first chapter of *The Interpretation of Dreams*, Freud gave a detailed survey of the findings of nineteenth-century experimental dream researchers. These researchers had devoted careful study to the possible connections between the mental content of dreams and the physical conditions of the dreamer's sleeping body. They had found, for example, that certain forms of external stimulus would frequently enter into the person's dream. If the researcher rang a bell near the ear of a sleeping person, the sound might appear in the person's dream as an alarm clock, or a fire engine, or a church bell. Similarly, the researchers found that certain internal stimuli would also enter into people's dreams. Being feverish might lead to a dream of walking through a hot desert; having a full bladder might produce a dream of watering flowers in a garden.

But after reviewing the work of these researchers, Freud essentially dismissed their findings as unimportant. He argued that such experiments, while interesting, really tell us nothing fundamental about the formation or functions of dreams. Why, he asked, does one person hear the stimulus of a ringing bell and dream of an alarm clock, while another person hearing the exact same stimulus dreams of a church bell? Why do some people fail to incorporate external stimuli like ringing bells into their dreams, and why do other people dream of alarm clocks and church bells without hearing any external stimuli? Because experimental researchers had failed to provide good answers to these questions, Freud decided that their work could not contribute anything of real value to the modern psychology of dreaming. He concluded, "what we are concerned with is not the origin of certain special dreams but the source that instigates the ordinary dreams of normal people" (1965a, 69).

Most psychologists following Freud agreed with this negative conclusion about the value of psychophysiological studies of dreaming. For the next five decades the primary focus of dream research was on the clinical work of psychotherapists. Because they have direct access to the intimate personal lives of their patients and clients, psychotherapists seemed to have the ideal background to answer basic questions about the nature of dreams.

But soon a serious problem arose with this exclusively clinical approach to dream psychology: every clinician seemed to come up with a different theory about the nature of dreaming. Alternative models, methods, and approaches multiplied rapidly. Rather than moving toward greater clarity and consensus, dream psychologists appeared to be moving ever farther apart, their theories increasingly contradicting one another.

A dramatic change in the history of twentieth-century dream psychology occurred in the 1950's, when sleep laboratory researchers discovered the phenomenon of rapid eye movement (REM) sleep and its associations with dreaming. Suddenly, the possibility opened up that dreaming could be objectively observed, precisely measured, and experimentally studied in a controlled laboratory situation. At long last it appeared that a truly scientific psychology of dreaming could be developed.

This chapter will describe the original research on REM sleep and will discuss how the subsequent explosion of sleep laboratory investigations of REM sleep has transformed the modern psychology of dreaming.

ASERINSKY AND KLEITMAN'S DISCOVERY OF REM SLEEP

Nathaniel Kleitman was a physiologist at the University of Chicago who had for many years been studying the nature of sleep, and particularly the effects of sleep deprivation. One of his students was Eugene Aserinsky, who was doing graduate work investigating aspects of attention in children. While collecting data for his research project, Aserinsky noticed one day that the children's eyes began shifting about very quickly beneath their lids whenever they lost attention and fell asleep.

These darting eye movements were completely different from the slow, rolling eye movements that researchers had long observed occurring at sleep onset.[1] Aserinsky mentioned his observations to Kleitman, and when they began more carefully studying the children they were surprised to find that these eye movements were very much like a person's eye movements while awake. Aserinsky and Kleitman conducted further experiments, and they soon learned that these periods of highly coordinated eye movements, which occurred in both children and adults, were accompanied by distinctive brain wave patterns, irregular breathing, and increased heart rate.

The results of their research were as clear as they were revolutionary: the brain does not simply turn off when a person goes to sleep, resting peacefully until it's turned back on in the morning. Aserinsky and Kleitman had found that at regular points during the night our brains become very active—indeed, sometimes more active than when we are awake. William Dement, a medical student who became a member of Kleitman's research team, coined the term "rapid eye movement sleep," or REM sleep, to designate this newly-discovered brain state. About Aserinsky and Kleitman's discovery Dement later wrote,

This was *the* breakthrough—the discovery that changed the course of sleep research from a relatively pedestrian inquiry into an intensely exciting endeavor pursued with great determination in laboratories and clinics all over the world. . . . For the first time we realized what has probably been true of man's sleep since he crawled out of the primordial slime. Man has *two* kinds of sleep. His nocturnal solitude contains two entirely different phenomena. (1972, 25)

Aserinsky and Kleitman published their initial findings in 1953 in the journal *Science*. They published a longer article in 1955, titled "Two Types of Ocular Motility Occurring in Sleep," in the *Journal of Applied Physiology*. Their 1955 article discussed the possibility that REM sleep is associated with dreaming. They reported that subjects who were awakened after a period of REM sleep gave detailed dream accounts twenty out of twenty-seven times; subjects who were awakened after a period of NREM (non-rapid eye movement) sleep gave dream accounts only four out of twenty-three times. Aserinsky and Kleitman concluded that "the evidence for the association of the rapid eye movements with dreaming, or at least the recall of dreaming, is strong" (1955, 8–9). They found that some of the dream reports following REM periods involved "strikingly vivid visual imagery," leading them to suggest that "it is indeed highly probable that rapid eye movements are directly associated with visual imagery in dreaming" (1955, 9).

EARLY RESEARCH ON REM AND NREM SLEEP

The first sleep laboratory studies following Aserinsky and Kleitman's original work concentrated on mapping out more carefully these new features of the terrain of sleep. Researchers soon determined that a typical night's sleep for an adult human follows a regular alteration of REM sleep and four stages of non-rapid eye movement (NREM) sleep. These different NREM stages are defined by their different percentages of brain wave activity. Sleeping individuals are said to "descend" through the four NREM stages in that their sleep becomes deeper, they become more remote from the external environment, and stronger stimuli are required to wake them up.

Figure 5.1
Sequences of States and Stages of Sleep on a Typical Night

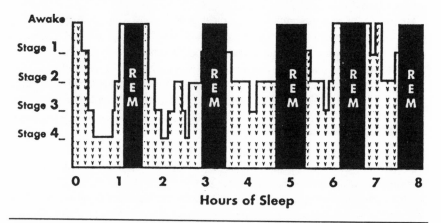

As shown in Figure 5.1, when people fall asleep they descend from stage 1 NREM to stage 2, stage 3, and finally stage 4. After being asleep for an hour or so, people will start moving "up" from stage 4 NREM to stage 3, then to stage 2, and then to stage 1 again. At this point, approximately ninety minutes after sleep onset, the first REM period of the night begins. Brain wave activity increases dramatically, muscle tone changes, heartbeat and respiration become irregular, and blood flow to the genitals increases (resulting in enlargement of the clitoris in women and erection of the penis in men). This first REM period lasts for perhaps ten minutes. People then descend again through the NREM stages, usually staying in stage 3 NREM sleep for a while, and perhaps making a brief return to stage 4, before rising up to the next REM period. Throughout the night this cyclic alteration between NREM and REM sleep continues, with an average of ninety minutes between the onset of one REM period and that of the next one. As the night goes on the REM periods increase in duration, and by the end of the night they may last as long as an hour. Conversely, the NREM periods become shorter. Stages 1, 3, and 4 more or less disappear, and the sleeper alternates almost exclusively between stage 2 sleep and REM until awakening. On average, then, adult humans experience four or five periods of REM sleep each night, or approximately one-quarter of their total sleep time.

Research by Dement and by Michel Jouvet, a French neurosurgeon, demon-strated that a very similar cycle of REM-NREM sleep alteration occurs in cats. Other sleep laboratory researchers soon confirmed that all mammals (with the apparent exceptions of the spiny anteater and the bottlenose dolphin [see Crick and Mitchison 1983, 114, and Long 1987, 820]) experience substantial amounts of REM sleep. Most reptiles appear to have NREM sleep but nothing like REM sleep; birds, according to Dement, "have very well developed NREM sleep, and show occasional, very brief (one second) episodes of what appears to be an evolutionary precursor of the REM period" (1972, 30).

Researchers also found that for many mammals the percentage of REM sleep is higher among newborns than among adults.[2] Newborn kittens, puppies, rats, and hamsters, for instance, have nothing but REM sleep. For human infants, at least 50 percent of their sleep is REM; in fact, REM periods have actually been detected in the sleep of human fetuses before birth. Sleep laboratory researchers have taken all this as strong evidence that REM sleep serves some evolutionary function in the activation and maturation of the brains of young mammals.

As researchers tried to understand the nature and possible functions of REM sleep, they conducted deprivation experiments to see what would happen if people were prevented from having any REM sleep at all. In these experiments subjects were allowed to sleep through the four NREM stages but were awakened every time they entered REM sleep. Dement conducted one of the first deprivation experiments, and he reported that his subjects became anxious, irritable, and unable to concentrate after five days of REM deprivation. He speculated that "if the dream suppression were carried on long enough, a serious disruption of the personality would result" (1960, 1707).

However, later experiments by Dement and others did not confirm the sugges-tion that depriving people of REM would cause terrible psychological damage. What these experiments did demonstrate, though, was a "rebound effect": a REM-deprived subject will, when allowed to sleep again through a night without interruption, experience a dramatic increase in REM sleep. Following a period of REM deprivation, a subject will in subsequent nights enter REM sleep more quickly and stay in it longer. Researchers have taken this as indicative of a strong physiological need for REM sleep. Interestingly, researchers have also conducted experiments depriving subjects of NREM sleep, and have found similar rebound effects. It seems that mammals need both REM sleep *and* NREM sleep.

Another set of sleep laboratory experiments on both humans and animals looked at the relationship of REM sleep to learning and information processing. For example, animals who underwent difficult learning tasks were found to have increased amounts of REM sleep the following nights. Likewise, humans who were faced with complex or stressful learning tasks experienced higher percent-ages of REM sleep. When their REM sleep was disrupted or entirely eliminated, both animals and humans were less able to retain newly learned information (see Smith 1993). Some researchers focused specifically on REM sleep and the processing of information with a high emotional charge. Ramon Greenberg and his colleagues conducted an experiment in which subjects were shown a stressful movie (a graphic portrayal of an autopsy). Half of the subjects were then REM-deprived the night following the movie, and half were awakened during NREM periods. When shown the movie a second time, the REM-deprived subjects reacted with markedly more anxiety than did the other subjects. Without the benefits of REM sleep, these subjects were evidently less able to manage the stress of a repeat viewing of the movie. Greenberg and his colleagues concluded that REM sleep seems to function in helping us emotionally process anxiety-provoking situations and experiences (Greenberg et al. 1972).

Another important research project, conducted by Rosalind Cartwright and her colleagues, focused on investigating the dream characteristics of people going through a major life change (in her study, women going through a divorce). She found that among the women who were not significantly depressed by their divorce, REM dreams were longer, had a wider time perspective, dealt with negative emotions, and portrayed the dreamer's self in marital roles. By contrast, among the women who were depressed by their divorce, REM dreams were less visual and storylike, had a narrower, past-oriented time frame, did not identify the dreamer with any marital roles, and generally avoided any mention of the divorce. When Cartwright did follow-up interviews with the depressed women, she found that as their waking moods improved their dream characteristics changed in the direction of the non-depressed women. She concluded that dreams definitely do respond to major events in waking life, and that "when affect levels in response to events are moderate, dream changes appear to be more adaptive than when events are accompanied by disruptively high affect levels" (Cartwright et al. 1984, 259).

The changes to modern psychological knowledge produced by the discovery of REM sleep cannot be overestimated. In the space of just a few years sleep laboratory researchers demonstrated that while we sleep our brains engage in a cyclical pattern of highly complex activities. These activities frequently become so intense that they are indistinguishable from the brain's activities while we are awake. Neuroscientist J. Allan Hobson, whose work will be discussed later in this chapter, has said that if sleep researchers had only the electroencephalogram (EEG) machines that measure brain wave patterns to go by, they would have difficulty in distinguishing the brain state associated with waking from the brain state associated with REM. "If we were not able to observe that a subject is behaviorally awake in the first case and sleeping in the second, the EEG alone would not be capable of indicating whether a subject is awake or [in REM sleep]" (1988, 136).

REM, NREM, AND DREAMING

The crucial question remains: what exactly does REM sleep have to do with dreaming? As noted above, Aserinsky and Kleitman's 1955 article argued that there is strong evidence that REM sleep and dreaming are associated. Kleitman and Dement published two articles in 1957 which indicated that subjects awakened immediately following a REM period reported dreams far more frequently than did subjects awakened during NREM sleep. Their findings gave rise to the belief that REM sleep and dreaming were identical, were *isomorphic*—we dream when we are in REM sleep, and we don't dream when we are in NREM sleep. Some researchers began to refer to REM sleep as "dreaming sleep."

But other researchers questioned this hasty assumption of REM-dreaming isomorphism. David Foulkes, who did his dissertation work in the University of Chicago's sleep laboratory, challenged the idea that NREM sleep is a dreamless void by raising the crucial issue of how researchers were defining the phenomenon "dreaming." When Foulkes awakened his subjects from NREM sleep, he asked them, "Was anything going through your mind?" rather than "Were you dreaming?" He found that more than 50 percent of the time subjects reported mental occurrences from NREM sleep with visual, auditory, and/or kinesthetic imagery (Foulkes 1962). Foulkes said that the NREM reports tended to be shorter, with less intense visual imagery, physical activity, and emotional involvement, than dream reports from REM sleep. However, he argued that many of the NREM mental occurrences could still plausibly be regarded as dreams; at the very least, they were legitimate phenomena of sleep and deserved study as such.

Other researchers confirmed Foulkes's findings. The two dreams quoted at the beginning of this chapter indicate the general differences that many studies found between the mental activities of NREM and REM sleep. In his book *Some Must Watch While Some Must Sleep* (1972) Dement concludes,

Compared with REM recall, NREM mentation is generally more poorly recalled, more like thinking and less like dreaming, less vivid, less visual, more conceptual, under greater volitional control, more plausible, more concerned with contemporary lives, occurring in lighter sleep, less emotional, and more pleasant. The impression is that NREM mentation resembles that large portion of our waking thought that wanders in a seemingly disorganized, drifting, nondirected fashion whenever we are not attending to external stimuli. (44)

But even this broad generalization that NREM reports are more thought-like and REM reports are more dream-like has been challenged by later research. While very vivid, elaborate dream narratives are rarely found during NREM, many NREM reports cannot be distinguished from REM reports. The differences, Foulkes has said, are distributional rather than categorical: the dream-like qualities of emotional intensity, visual vividness, physical activity, and so forth, occur on average more frequently in REM reports than in NREM reports. But many REM reports do *not* possess such qualities, while many NREM reports *do*.

The exact relationship between REM sleep, NREM sleep, and dreaming continues to be studied, and heatedly debated, by sleep laboratory researchers (See Moffitt et al. 1993 for a good review of the literature surrounding this debate).

Currently, almost all researchers will agree on at least these points:

- REM sleep is not identical with dreaming.
- NREM sleep is not a dreamless void.
- Mental activities occur through all stages of the sleep cycle.

From all the studies that researchers have performed since Aserinsky and Kleitman's breakthrough discovery, it seems certain that REM sleep has some special connection to dreaming. However, it remains unclear what precisely this connection may be.

HOBSON'S ACTIVATION-SYNTHESIS HYPOTHESIS

The most determined effort to specify the connections between REM sleep and dreaming has been made by J. Allan Hobson, a neuroscientist at Harvard University. First in a 1977 article, "The Brain as a Dream-State Generator: An Activation-Synthesis Hypothesis of the Dream Process" (co-authored with Robert W. McCarley), and then in his 1988 book *The Dreaming Brain*, Hobson sets out to demonstrate that the neurological activity of the brain during REM sleep creates both the sense and the nonsense of dreams.

From the opening pages of *The Dreaming Brain* it is clear that Hobson is writing directly against Freud and the psychoanalytic theory of dreams. But Hobson is attacking not only Freud, for he sees psychoanalysis as the culmination of a long history of dream interpretation, which he calls "the prophetic tradition." According to this tradition dreams are believed to be caused by external agencies (e.g., gods or spirits), to contain secret, coded messages, and to require elaborate interpretations by special authorities. In Hobson's view, psychoanalysis is but the latest carrier of this time-honored tradition, with Freud claiming that dreams come from the mysterious unconscious, are deviously disguised wish-fulfillments, and cannot be understood without the aid of a skilled psychoanalyst. Hobson believes that in psychoanalysis the language has changed, but that the essentially superstitious, prophetic perspective remains the same.

Rather than obeying the dogmas of this prophetic tradition, stretching from the Bible to Freud, Hobson says he will follow the tradition of science, "in which experimental accomplices or instrumentation have been used to make the study of dreams more systematic and more objective" (1988, 12). His approach is to provide a scientific explanation for how dreams are formed; with that explanation as a basis, he will be able to show what dreams mean.

Drawing on modern neurological research, Hobson says that a constant competition between groups of neurons in the brain leads to the cycles of waking, sleeping, and dreaming:

REM sleep and dreaming are the result of temporary domination of one neuronal population over another. Victorious is a troop of reticular-formation neurons concentrated mainly in the pontine portion of the brain stem; owing to their fusillades of firing in association with REM-sleep events, these pontine reticular neurons are likely to play the executive role in the generation of REM sleep and dreaming. Sharing the white flag of temporary surrender is a population of aminergic neurons . . . ; hardly a shot is fired by this neuronal phalanx during REM sleep. (183)

The key conclusion that Hobson draws from this model, which he calls "the reciprocal-interaction model of REM-sleep generation," is that REM sleep is caused by neurological processes that are involuntary, cyclical, and rooted in our physiological nature.

To account for how the activity of neuronal populations in the brain during REM sleep is transformed into the psychological experience of dreaming, Hobson offers the "activation-synthesis hypothesis of dreaming." This hypothesis suggests that after neuronal processes have activated REM sleep, higher brain functions work to synthesize the essentially random input as well as it can, with dreams as the result. Hobson says, "the activation-synthesis hypothesis assumes that dreams are as meaningful as they can be under the adverse working conditions of the brain in REM sleep. The activated brain-mind does its best to attribute meaning to the internally generated signals" (214). In the synthesis stage of dream formation the mind makes sense of the nonsensical, random neurological activity, creating meanings where there were none before.

Although Hobson admits that we still know far too little about how the synthesis process actually works, he claims that his activation-synthesis hypothesis can account for the most important formal features of dreaming. For example, his hypothesis explains the predominantly visual character of dreams as the result of certain neuronal processes of REM sleep which stimulate visual receptors in the brain, leading the mind to think it is seeing external objects, characters, and settings (211). Likewise, Hobson's hypothesis regards the strong emotional content of many dreams as the product of emotional systems in the brain which become randomly activated during REM sleep, spontaneously making us feel angry, or sad, or excited; our mind responds to these sudden emotional upsurges by weaving together images and stories that try to make sense of the feelings (213). The distortions that are so common in dreams occur because the mind simply cannot make any real coherence or meaning out of the random, bizarre data that is continuously generated by the brain during REM sleep. Hobson and McCarley say in their 1977 paper, "such features as scene shifts, time compression, personal condensations, splitting, and symbol formation may be directly isomorphic with the state of the nervous system during dreaming sleep. In other words, the forebrain may be making the best of a bad job in producing even partially coherent dream imagery from the relatively noisy signals sent up to it from the brain stem" (1977, 1347).

The role of synthesis in dream formation reveals, Hobson believes, an essentially human capacity to imagine and create: his theory "sees the brain as so inexorably bent upon the quest for meaning that it attributes and even creates meaning when there is little or none to be found in the data it is asked to process" (1988, 15). Hobson says the brain labors, in sleeping and in waking, to create a meaningful integration of its experience, "even if it must resort to creative storytelling" (219). Indeed, the utterly chaotic neural firings that bombard us in REM sleep often confound all ordinary means of organizing our perceptions, leading to extraordinary attempts at synthesis. Hobson grants that perhaps the "symbolic, prophetic character [of dreams] arises from the integrative strain of this synthetic effort. The brain-mind may need to call upon its deepest myths to find a narrative frame that can contain the data" (214).

A crucial consequence that Hobson draws from the activation-synthesis hypothesis is that the meaning of dreams is not hidden or coded, but rather is clear, transparent, and present right on the surface of the dream: "for activation-synthesis the dream as reported is the transparent and directly legible product of an unusual mode of information processing" (217). Whatever meaning there is to a dream, it comes during the process of synthesis, with no masks, deceptions, or codings. Dreams have their origins in purely random neural activity; this proves, Hobson believes, that the prophetic tradition's demand for complex interpretations by authoritative specialists is groundless.

Hobson presents his own dreams and the dreams of "The Engine Man" (a middle-aged scientist who, in 1939, carefully recorded 233 of his dreams in a journal) as evidence to show that the meanings of dreams are in fact clear, undistorted, and readily understood. With his own dreams, Hobson finds that his feelings, wishes, perceptions, and thoughts are all easily recognized; "this all seems very transparent to me. Almost naked" (233). Activation-synthesis can account for many of the strange features of his dreams, and his own common sense explains the rest. In *The Dreaming Brain* Hobson recounts one of his own dreams as a way of clarifying the contrast between his interpretive position and that of "Freudian orthodoxy":

My wife, Joan, and I are at the Museum of Fine Arts in Boston to attend a concert in the larger Remus auditorium. It is someone (perhaps John Gibbons) playing a Mozart piano (concerto?) on a large Steinway (no orchestra, but image vague anyway). (The piano is reminiscent of the large Steinway grand in the great hall of the Phillips Collection in Washington, which I visited the previous Saturday.) As is usual on such 'museum' occasions, I am restive, feeling like the third wheel on Joan's business bicycle, and hence inattentive.

I decide to explore and go down to the smaller, older theater (near the Egyptian sarcophagi). This theater is now limited to small lectures but was, twenty years ago, the place where, as young members, Joan and I attended museum programs of the type that are now in Remus, and now under Joan's direction.

I hear the music and the faint bustle of excitement. Opening the door a crack, I am amazed to realize that Mozart himself is on stage, playing the same concerto (again without orchestra) on an antique harpsichord from the museum collection (not the Mozart piano forte). Although the door is open only for an instant, I notice Mozart's rich red brocaded frock coat (the curlicues are gold-embossed) and his white powdered wig. He has a beatific smile, and the arpeggios stream through the door into my ear. I also notice that Mozart has gotten a bit overweight, and wonder why.

I close the door with a shhh!, and try to figure out how to tell Joan of my discovery." (220)

A psychoanalytic interpretation of this dream, Hobson says, would focus on Mozart as symbolizing a powerful and greatly admired male, for example Hobson's father. But an interpretation based on the activation-synthesis hypothesis would begin with the scientific fact that the neurological activity of his brain during REM sleep had led him to create a dream that eventually circled around the themes of concern, Mozart, and museum. Hobson admits that the dream could have meanings in the psychoanalytic sense—he says "I *am* ambitious. I *do* admire Mozart. I *would*, consciously, like to be as brilliant as Mozart" (222). Nevertheless, he insists that a simpler, more common-sensical interpretation of the dream is that Mozart is just a mentally-created image of Mozart, nothing more. *The Dreaming Brain* ends with a discussion of the basic functions of REM sleep. Hobson says that REM sleep helps the brain maintain its basic neural circuits: our regular, day-to-day activities do not draw on all of our brain's potential abilities, so REM sleep works to exercise the brain, regularly activating all its neural circuitry in the physically safe environment of sleep (the only neural systems not activated during REM sleep are those responsible for critical attention in waking life, because these systems are very sensitive and easily exhausted). Hobson likens our brain to a car sitting in a garage—we need to "rev our cerebral motor" at least once a day so that it stays in good working order.

Hobson believes that when the neurological basis of REM sleep is properly understood, it becomes clear that dreams are simply the mind's creative attempts at making sense of the random neural activities of the brain in REM sleep. Dreams do not come from spirits, gods, nor even the dark wishes of the unconscious; dreams come from the brain, and they highlight the fundamentally artistic nature of human beings, our intense determination to make meaning, even where none really exists. While he agrees with Freud that dreams may be interpreted for personal meanings, Hobson says his position "echoes Jung's notion of dreams as transparently meaningful. . . . I wish again to emphasize strongly that I am not asserting that dreams are either meaningless or unworthy of clinical attention. On the contrary . . . the meaning of dreams is for me transparent rather than concealed, since fundamentally incoherent cognitive elements are synthesized in a personally meaningful way. This 'meaning-added' process is the exact opposite of that envisaged by psychoanalysis, which asserts that fully coherent and deeply meaningful ideas (the latent dream content) must be degraded and disguised (by the dream work), resulting in an incoherent product (the manifest content) acceptable to consciousness. For me, the manifest content is the dream: there is no other dream." (12, 258).

CRICK AND MITCHISON'S REVERSE LEARNING THEORY

In 1983 an article titled "The Function of Dream Sleep" was published in the journal *Nature* by Francis Crick, the Nobel Prize winning co-discoverer of the DNA molecule, and Graeme Mitchison, a neuroscientist at the Salk Institute in La Jolla, California. Based upon their research into the workings of the mammalian cerebral cortex, Crick and Mitchison offer a new explanation for the function of REM sleep and a new view of the nature of dreams. They start with Hobson's notion of REM sleep as a means of maintaining good cerebral functioning, but they take it in a quite different direction. Crick and Mitchison argue that rather than just giving the brain's neural circuitry a little exercise each night, REM sleep focuses specifically on eliminating potentially damaging patterns of brain functioning.

Crick and Mitchison begin their argument with the observation that the brain's network of interconnected cells is so complex and so sensitive that "unwanted or 'parasitic' modes of behavior" can easily take hold when it is disturbed either by the brain's natural growth or by external experience (1983, 111). To perform as well as it does, the mammalian brain must have some way of ridding itself of these negative behavioral modes, and Crick and Mitchison claim that REM sleep serves this function: "We propose that such modes are detected and suppressed by a special mechanism which operates during REM sleep and has the character of an active process which is, loosely speaking, the opposite of learning. We call this 'reverse learning' or 'unlearning'" (111).

Although Crick and Mitchison admit that their reverse-learning theory is quite speculative and extremely difficult to test, they insist that it makes sense of two basic sleep laboratory facts: REM sleep is especially prominent in infancy; and almost all of our dreams are, in ordinary circumstances, forgotten. Infants need so much REM sleep because their brains are developing at a rapid rate, and many faulty or improper neural connections are accidentally being made. REM sleep helps in the necessary process of cleaning out those faulty connections, allowing the more useful ones to be strengthened and built up. We still need REM sleep in adulthood because even mature brains occasionally suffer from the accidental development of parasitic modes of behavior, requiring the regular activation of that neural self-cleaning process. Regarding the fact that most of our dreams are forgotten, Crick and Mitchison say this occurs for the simple reason that dreams are *meant* to be forgotten—the focus of REM sleep dreaming is on precisely those neural patterns that the brain needs to eliminate. Crick and Mitchison go on to suggest that the practice of dream interpretation may inadvertently reverse the function of REM sleep: "In this model, attempting to remember one's dreams should perhaps not be encouraged, because such remembering may help to retain patterns of thought which are better forgotten. These are the very patterns the organism was attempting to damp down" (114).

THE "LAB EFFECT"

Throughout the history of sleep laboratory investigations of dreaming, researchers have debated the question of how much influence the laboratory setting itself has on the subject's dreams. When people come to sleep in the laboratory, they lie down in a strange bed and have wires attached to their heads, torsos, and even genitals; they know that other people are going to be watching them all night long, and they know that they will suddenly be awakened a number of times during the night and asked by strangers to answer various questions. It's only natural that the experience of sleeping in a laboratory would generate anxiety in the people who serve as research subjects, and that their anxiety would influence their dreams. For example, research subjects frequently have dreams that incorporate explicit features of the laboratory setting—the wires, the researchers, the bedroom, the hospital, and so on. They also frequently have dreams relating more obliquely to the lab setting, such as dreams of taking a test, or talking with a doctor, or being paid to do a special job.

As part of a 1962 sleep laboratory study by R. Whitman and his colleagues at a veteran's hospital in Cincinnati the researchers tried to soothe the subjects' fears by showing them around the lab, carefully explaining what the EEG machines did, and answering all their questions about the research project. However, Whitman concluded that despite these efforts to make the subjects more comfortable, the lab effect on their dreams remained strong:

It is clear in this study that neither reassurance about the [laboratory] apparatus nor repeated episodes of exposure to the apparatus were sufficient to decrease anxiety about the experimental situation, even over a period of four weeks. Surface cooperativeness and surface placidity may well hide massive fears and anxiety reactions which would affect physiological, biochemical and, of course, psychological measurements. (Whitman et al. 1962, 439)

A few years later Calvin Hall and Robert Van de Castle (whose work will be described in the next chapter) compared dreams reported in the sleep lab with dreams reported in a home setting. They found that the home dreams had more aggression, friendliness, sex, misfortune, and good fortune; overall, the home dreams seemed to have a greater "dramatic quality" than did the lab dreams (Van de Castle 1994, 284). Commenting on these findings, Hall says that "although there is no way of knowing at the present time what 'typical dream life' is like, it is a plausible assumption that it will not be found in a laboratory setting no matter how normal the environment provided the subject" (1967, 206). In Van de Castle's book *Our Dreaming Mind* he notes that nocturnal emissions, or "wet dreams," are extremely rare among subjects sleeping in a laboratory setting, which he takes as further evidence that the lab has an inhibiting effect on people's dreams (1994, 237).

Ernest Hartmann's research on nightmares (also to be discussed in the next chapter) gives still another perspective on the power of the lab effect. He found that "nightmares almost never occur spontaneously in the sleep laboratory in normal subjects, and even persons who report frequent nightmares at home have much fewer in the laboratory" (1984, 37). Hartmann suggests that when people sleep in a lab they feel a sense of protection, a sense that the trained research staff will prevent any harm from coming to them in the night.

Taken together, these research findings indicate that the sleep laboratory has the effect of homogenizing people's dreams—making it less likely that people will experience, remember, and/or report their more extraordinary, emotionally intense dreams. Certain types of dreams—highly sexual dreams, highly aggressive dreams, nightmares, and perhaps other unusual dream types—seem to elude capture by the machinery of the sleep lab. This means that studies relying on laboratory data alone may not give a truly accurate and comprehensive picture of human dreaming experience.

Nevertheless, other researchers have argued that the lab effect can be minimized and that the sleep laboratory remains the best tool available for investigating the nature of dreaming. Research by Dement, for example, has shown that after their first night in the lab subjects usually incorporate fewer elements from the experimental situation into their dreams (Dement et al. 1965). As a consequence, for years now almost all sleep lab studies have let their subjects sleep through the first night without any interruptions, to allow the people a chance to get comfortable in the lab setting.

David Foulkes argues vigorously that proper research methods can eliminate all negative influences due to the lab effect, and he goes on to assert that the sleep laboratory is an indispensable device for investigating dreams. In his research on children's dreams Foulkes insists that only dream reports gathered in the laboratory are sufficiently representative for the purposes of scientific dream study. He rejects investigations based on spontaneously remembered dreams from home settings because "the sampling bias [is] horrendous" (1982, 175)—the factors influencing the quantity and quality of children's dreams recalled at home are so numerous and so unpredictable that no legitimate conclusions can be based on them:

What conclusions about the workings of the child's mind in sleep, or about individual differences in these workings, could possibly be based on nonrandom, incomplete sampling of this kind? The dream student's choice cannot be dreams which are reported "truly spontaneously"; the only reasonable question facing such a student is where and how to study dreams deliberately and systematically. . . . [S]ince the undoubted gains in representative sampling in the laboratory are in no significant way jeopardized by losses in the representativeness of the dreams being sampled, the most reasonable answer to this question is: "in the laboratory." (1982, 136)

As with so many issues in modern dream psychology, the nature and significance of the "lab effect" continues to be debated.

THE SLEEP LABORATORY'S ANSWERS TO THE THREE BASIC QUESTIONS

Formation

Sleep laboratory researchers have found that almost all mammals experience the regular and cyclic occurrence of rapid eye movement (REM) sleep, when the brain becomes highly active, heart rate and respiration increase, and the eyes jerkily dart about underneath their lids. The typical sleeping pattern for humans involves the alternation between REM and four stages of NREM sleep. On average, adult humans spend a quarter of their sleep time in REM; newborn humans (and the newborns of many mammals) experience a far higher percentage of REM sleep. After being deprived of REM sleep, people experience a rebound effect in which they have more REM sleep on the nights following the deprivation. REM sleep seems to play a role in the learning of new information and the processing of emotionally significant events from daily life. Sleep laboratory researchers do not, however, agree on how closely REM sleep should be identified with dreaming. This makes it difficult to derive from their work any clear, definite answers to the three basic questions about dreaming. At present, it appears that dreams reported from REM sleep tend to be more vivid, more emotional, and more active than dreams reported from the four stages of NREM sleep. Thus, the strongest conclusion that sleep laboratory researchers have made regards the question of formation: dreaming seems in some important way to be generated and shaped by the complex neural activities of the brain during REM sleep. And because all humans experience REM sleep, laboratory research indicates that all humans dream every single night, whether or not they remember having dreamed when they wake up.

Function

On the question of dream function, sleep laboratory researchers have suggested that dreaming may promote the early growth and adaptation of the brain; may help people respond effectively to novel, complex, and/or anxiety-provoking experiences; and may generally work to process new information learned during the day. The fact that almost all mammals experience REM sleep, while reptiles and birds generally do not, indicates that dreaming may have some evolutionary value.

Interpretation

Few sleep laboratory researchers devote sustained attention to the question of how to interpret dreams. Hobson makes the most noteworthy effort to correlate scientific knowledge about REM sleep with method of interpreting the meanings of particular dreams. He says that every dream is a product of the random, involuntary neural activities of the brain during REM sleep: the mind struggles to make sense of these neural activities by creating images and narratives, some of which may have personal meanings for the individual. For Hobson, dream interpretation is simply a matter of sifting these bits of personal meaning out of the bizarre, nonsensical imagery that comes with all dreaming.

NOTES

1. Hobson remarks that Aserinsky's observations of children's sleep made it particularly likely for him to notice these eye movements, because "unlike adults, children often enter the REM phase immediately at sleep onset; and these sleep-onset REM periods are especially likely to occur during daytime naps" (1988, 140).

2. This is true for "altricial" mammals, that is, those animals that are born immature, such as humans and rats. "Precocial" mammals that are born functional, like most grazing animals (cattle, deer, giraffes), have their adult levels of REM right from birth.

Chapter 6

Experimental Psychology and Dreaming

Mummy made a big, green statue out of leaves. A fox came and knocked it over by pushing its head into the leaves. I was frightened of the fox and went back into mummy's inside to hide. Then he couldn't catch me.

Five-year old girl, in Piaget 1962, 178

I remember driving up a hill on a paved road. It was a steep hill, probably in Maine. The road made a right hand turn, but I kept right on going in the same direction I was going. I was going up a trail that was very steep. I kept right on going till I reached the top of this hill. There was no road up there, just a trail and a lot of rocks. I felt rather foolish driving all the way up, and I came back down. Then the setting changes. It was flat-seeming, like Florida is. Then I stopped to see one of my customers, but this is no customer that I recognized. As I saw she was just a customer, I never even got out of the car. She just came to the car window and I rolled it down to talk to her. She was a woman about 45 and had brown hair. I don't remember the conversation. It was pleasant though. It only lasted a few minutes. I drove on and that's about all I can remember.

Twenty-one-year old man, in Domhoff 1996 269–270

Experimental psychology is the systematic empirical study of the mind. Its primary subjects are the nature and development of perception, language, reason, memory, and imagination. Many experimental psychologists have taken a deep interest in dreaming, investigating it as a possible source of valuable evidence regarding the basic structures and workings of the mind. How is dreaming like, and unlike, waking consciousness? What special cognitive operations are involved in constructing the experiences that occur during sleep? How are the images and settings of dreams formed? Where does the spoken dialogue come from? Which parts of dreams are based on old memories, and which parts (if any) are freshly created? How are people and objects from waking life transformed in dreams? What role in dreaming is played by the complex symbolic operations at work in our thought and language? How are the dreams of adults related to the dreams of children? Does a capacity for dreaming develop in tandem with the general cognitive development of a maturing human?

In recent years a great deal of high-quality experimental psychological research on dreaming has been published. Because no single chapter could adequately survey all of the available material, this chapter concentrates on the more limited task of profiling the pioneering researchers in this area, outlining their major projects, and describing their responses to the dream theorists who preceded them. The common theme in the work of these researchers is that dreaming is a product of the human mind, and should thus be studied in the same systematic, empirical way as that in which other forms of mental functioning have been investigated. In the view of these researchers, clinicians from Freud onward have failed to use adequate scientific methodologies in their dream research; and while psychophysi-ologists in the sleep laboratory have performed genuinely scientific experiments, they have focused almost exclusively on the nature of REM sleep rather than on dreaming per se. The aim of experimental psychologists has been to fill this research void by performing controlled scientific examinations on how and why the human mind creates dreams.

JEAN PIAGET ON PLAY, DREAMS, AND IMITATION IN CHILDHOOD

By all accounts, Swiss psychologist Jean Piaget is one of the great figures of modern experimental psychology. Originally trained in biology, Piaget turned early in his career to the study of psychology, specifically to the development of human intelligence. His goal was to integrate the theoretical speculations of philosophers and psychoanalysts with empirical data gained from careful scientific research. Over the next several decades Piaget produced a vast number of books and articles that examined many different facets of cognitive development.

Drawing on his background in biology, Piaget defined intelligence as an organism's ability to adapt to its environment—meaning that human language, reason, and imagination could be understood and analyzed as special tools that help us adapt successfully to the world in which we live. He argued that the intellectual growth of children should be a primary subject of psychological research, because in children we find the evolutionary origins of all forms of mature adult cognitive functioning.

Piaget's chief study of children's dreams is *Play, Dreams, and Imitation in Childhood*, originally published in 1946. In this work he examines how children struggle to adapt to the world around them. Piaget says their efforts follow two basic strategies: accommodation and assimilation. The purest form of accommodation is imitation, when children try to repeat exactly what they've seen or experienced in the world; through imitation they try to accommodate themselves to the demands of objective reality. The purest form of assimilation is play, when children create and control their own imaginary world; through play they try to assimilate objective reality to the demands of their subjective wishes and desires. By means of these two strategies of accommodation and assimilation children can gradually develop a realistic view of external reality, a strong individual ego, and a balanced, well-adjusted relationship between objective and subjective worlds.

Piaget regards children's dreaming as a continuation of the kind of symbolic play that is so common between the ages of three and five, and he identifies a number of similarities between the two phenomena. First, both dreaming and playing express children's basic physical and emotional desires, and they create imaginary fulfillments of those desires. Second, both often take a painful happening from the child's life and give it a different, happier ending. Third, both use simple forms of primary symbolism, which refer more or less directly to conscious thoughts (e.g., relating to common daily events and experiences). And fourth, both occasionally use more complex forms of secondary symbolism, which refer to deeply unconscious feelings and wishes (e.g., relating to the child's body, to emotions toward family members, to anxieties about childbirth, etc.). Piaget considers the five-year old girl's dream quoted at the beginning of this chapter an excellent example of how children use secondary symbolism to express unconscious desires. He says the girl

had asked shortly before [having the dream] how a statue of greenish bronze had been made, and she was also afraid that the foxes in the neighborhood might kill the animals she was rearing. But whatever the assimilations may be which would explain these images, the fact remains that [the girl], when frightened by the fox coming to destroy the statue, felt in her dream that the safest thing for her to do was to return to her mother's womb. (1962, 181)

The occurrence of nightmares reveals the only real difference between children's playing and dreaming, Piaget concludes. Fears and anxieties are commonly expressed in both playing and dreaming, "but in play there is always more or less conscious control, while in dreams control is more difficult, because the situation is assimilated to more deeply-seated schemas, i.e., to a more remote past" (180).

Piaget rejects Freud's theory that dreams are intentionally disguised by a censoring mechanism within the mind. Instead, he aligns himself with Jung's view that the symbolic images of dreams reflect basic mental patterns and structures common to all humans.[1] Although Piaget disagrees with Jung's claim that certain symbolic contents are inherited (and thus agrees with Freud that the capacity for symbolism originates anew in each individual), he does say we should accept Jung's basic notion that there is a level of primitive symbolic thought in each person's mind. However, to explain the origins and operations of this level of thought, Piaget argues that

we must come back to the child's visible and analysable psycho-genetic development. We are indebted to Freud for confining the problem of unconscious symbolism to the field of individual evolution. Once the idea of disguise is removed, symbolism can, thanks to the truly primitive character of the mechanisms of the child's thought, acquire the same degree of generality that Jung found in his hypothesis of a "collective unconscious." (198)

The ultimate goal of cognitive development, Piaget says, is to reach an equilibrium between the two strategies of accommodation and assimilation, a point of balance he calls "intelligent adaptation" (86). Healthy development requires that the distorted, egocentric fantasies of playing and dreaming become integrated with the individual's perceptions of and experiences with objective reality. When this occurs, playing and dreaming are transformed into the power of "creative imagination," a power which both broadens and stimulates the further growth of human intelligence in adulthood.

CALVIN HALL AND CONTENT ANALYSIS

Calvin Hall was an American psychologist whose prolific dream research began in the 1940s and continued until his death in 1985. He developed a means of studying dreams, the content analysis method, that has become one of the most influential and widely practiced techniques for the experimental study of dreams. Hall presented his research and theories in three major books: *The Meaning of Dreams*, first published in 1953 and revised in 1966, *The Content Analysis of Dreams*, co-authored with Robert Van de Castle in 1966, and *The Individual and His Dreams*, co-authored with Vernon Nordby in 1972.

The human fascination with dreams has led to many attempts to explain them, Hall says. The origin of dreams, for example, "has been attributed to such diverse sources as the absence of bed covers or the presence of spirits" (Hall and Van de Castle 1966, ix). Hall grants that Freud's dream theory went a long way toward providing a rational explanation of dreams, but that since Freud little real progress has been made: "it is true that others have advanced different theoretical interpretations of what constitutes the hidden message within dreams, but the methodology of investigating dreams has remained fixed at a qualitative stage of development" (Hall and Van de Castle 1966, ix).

Hall tries to advance the scientific study of dreams by developing the quantitative method of content analysis. This method involves taking a written dream report and breaking its content down into certain structural elements (the five basic categories Hall uses are setting, characters, interactions, objects, and emotions). These elements are then converted into numbers and statistically compared to large bodies of data gained from other dream reports. With this method, researchers are able to minimize the influence of subjective biases and develop conclusions that are sound, easily replicable, and clearly communicable.

A twenty-one-year old male college student, who was unmarried and who worked part-time as a Fuller Brush salesman, reported the following dream:

I was in a classroom teaching young women several things about cosmetics, hair care, etc. I remember getting into a big discussion on the virtues of natural hair brushes vs. nylon ones and the correct way to brush hair. The class was about 30 women about age 18 in a classroom much like we had in high school (fixed desks, and old building). The women all paid attention and discussed things well. (Domhoff 1996, 267–268)

According to the Hall and Van de Castle system this dream would be scored as follows. The characters in the dream are the dreamer and a group of adult females unfamiliar to the dreamer. The seven objects are the classroom and the old building (coded as two architectural objects of a vocational nature), the cosmetics, natural hair brushes, nylon brushes, and desks (coded as four household objects), and the hair (coded as a part of the body, specifically the head). The dream's setting is indoors, in a place of uncertain familiarity to the dreamer. The only social interaction is a friendly one, with the dreamer teaching the women about personal grooming. The only activity in the dream is a mutual verbal discussion between the dreamer and the group of women. There are no scorable emotions (i.e., anger, apprehension, happiness, sadness, confusion) in this dream (Domhoff 1996, 268–269).

Once a dream like this is scored by the Hall and Van de Castle system, it can be quantitatively compared to a series of other dreams reported by the same individual (the second dream quoted at the beginning of the chapter is also from this man). Examining a long series of dreams enables researchers to determine such facts as the average number of objects in the individual's dreams, the frequency of indoor versus outdoor settings, the presence or absence of certain emotions, the emotional quality of male-female interactions, and so forth. And when the dream scores of large groups of people are gathered and analyzed, researchers can quantitatively examine the differences in dream content between children and adults, between men and women, and between various social and ethnic groups (e.g., between Americans and Japanese, between blacks and whites, between members of modern industrial societies and members of small tribal communities).

Hall acknowledges that the content analysis method does not ask for any personal associations from the dreamer, as Freud, Jung, and many other psychologists insist is necessary for any legitimate study of dream content. But Hall replies that the reported "manifest" dream has great psychological significance apart from any personal associations, and he disputes Freud's distinction between the manifest and latent contents of dreams:

It could be said that there is no such thing as the latent content of a dream. A dream is a manifest experience, and what is latent lies outside the dream and in the verbal material that the dreamer reports when he is asked to free associate to features of the reported dream. How the psychoanalyst arrives at the 'true meaning' or interpretation of the dream from the verbalized associations is more of an art than a technique. This art may be of the utmost value in the therapeutic situation, but being a private, subjective type of activity it is of no direct value for research. (Hall and Van de Castle 1966, 20)

However helpful personal associations may be for the interpretation of dreams in clinical psychotherapy, in Hall's view they add nothing to objective scientific research on dreams.

Based on his content analysis method, Hall develops the theory that dreams are essentially projections of the mind which represent the subjective reality of the dreamer. Hall expands on Freud's fundamental claim that dreams reveal our unconscious instinctual impulses: Hall says dreams do more than tell us that a person has sexual and aggressive impulses, "they tell us what a person *thinks* about these basic impulses, what people they are directed against, and how they can best be satisfied" (Hall 1966, 70). For Hall, the symbols that appear in dreams are a kind of mental shorthand that help to express the person's thoughts (and not hide them, as Freud taught):

Dreaming is a form of thinking and thinking consists of formulating conceptions or ideas. When one dreams, his conceptions are turned into pictures. The images of a dream are the concrete embodiments of the dreamer's thoughts; these images give visible expression to that which is invisible, namely, conceptions. Accordingly the true referrent of any dream symbol is not an object or activity, it is always an idea in the mind of the dreamer. (1966, 95–96)

In *The Individual and His Dreams* Hall says that content analysis has demonstrated a simple truth about dreams. There is a close correspondence between people's dreams and their waking-life acts, thoughts, and beliefs. He calls this the "continuity hypothesis" of dreams, which asserts that "the world of dreaming and the world of waking are one" (Hall and Nordby 1972, 104). People generally dream about the same people they interact with in waking-life; they dream about the same places, the same objects, the same activities. The wishes and fears that appear in dreams are the same as those that determine waking-life thought and behavior. Hall says that while a few dreams obviously deviate from waking life experiences, content analysis has proven that people's dreaming lives are on average thoroughly continuous with their waking lives.

An interesting finding of Hall's dream research regards differences in dream content among men and women. He and other investigators using the content analysis method have found that women's dreams on average include more indoor settings, more friendly interactions, and more characters who are familiar to the dreamer; men's dreams on average contain more outdoor settings, more aggression, and more characters who are strangers to the dreamer. Most significantly, Hall found that in men's dreams almost two-thirds of the characters are males, and only one-third females; by contrast, women's dreams contain an equal number of male and female figures. Hall termed this a "ubiquitous sex difference" because dozens of research studies on many different groups of subjects have replicated this sizable disparity in the percentage of male and female characters in men's and women's dreams (Hall and Domhoff 1963a). Researchers are still investigating whether this gender difference in dream content is a product of physiology, or of culture, or of some combination of the two (Van de Castle 1994, 318–328).

Although its primary aim is to increase scientific knowledge about the workings of the human mind, the content analysis method does offer a means of personal dream interpretation. The key, Hall says, is always to analyze a series of dreams, because this makes it quite easy to identify the larger patterns of meaning that are woven through each individual dream. With this approach to dream interpretation, no special theoretical knowledge or technical skills are required:

The dreams read like chapters in a book. When put together in order as we have done there is organization, unity, and coherence among the dreams. Each dream complements or supplements the other dreams of the series. There is very little left to guesswork since what may seem ambiguous or hidden in one dream is revealed in another dream. Dream interpretation based upon a series of dreams can be very precise and objective if one approaches the task in a scientific manner. (Hall 1966, 84–85)

Among the many important research studies that have been performed using the Hall and Van de Castle system, one deserves special mention here. G. William Domhoff, who was one of Hall's closest colleagues, has written a sweeping summary of content analysis research on dreams titled *Finding Meaning in Dreams: A Quantitative Approach* (1996). In the concluding chapter of this book Domhoff examines what he calls the *repetition dimension* in dreams. By studying recurrent dreams, the nightmares of trauma victims, the widespread "typical" dreams of flying, falling, and so on, and the repeated elements in long series of dreams from one individual, Domhoff finds that repetition is a major feature all across the spectrum of dream content. He says that the repetition dimension is further evidence for Hall's continuity hypothesis, showing that people generally dream about the ongoing personal concerns and interests of their lives, and that people's dreams are surprisingly similar to their waking life thoughts and feelings. Domhoff argues that "no theory of dreams [should] be taken seriously if it cannot deal with the repetition dimension we show to be very prominent in dreams and dream content" (1996, 186).

DAVID FOULKES ON DREAMING AND LANGUAGE

As mentioned in the previous chapter, David Foulkes was originally trained in the sleep laboratory at the University of Chicago, where he performed important research on the relations between REM and NREM sleep. But Foulkes gradually became convinced that psychophysiological studies of REM and NREM sleep could not answer key questions about how the mind forms dreams. He decided that the best hope of answering these questions would come from using the latest models and methodologies of cognitive psychology, especially the recent findings that cognitive psychologists have made about the development of language. In three major books—*A Grammar of Dreams* (1978b), *Children's Dreams: Longitudinal Studies* (1982), and *Dreaming: A Cognitive-Psychological Analysis* (1985)—as well as in dozens of articles, Foulkes has argued that modern dream psychology must work to bring its research efforts more fully into the mainstream of cognitive psychology.

Foulkes's basic stance toward the psychological study of dreams is well stated in this passage, from the first chapter of *A Grammar of Dreams*:

One major obstacle to a full-fledged acceptance of dreaming as thinking is our reluctance to take responsibility for our dreams. Among many lay people and students of psychology this reluctance often takes the form of a belief in the supernatural (e.g., religious, telepathic) determination of dream content. For those who think of themselves as scientists, however, there always has been a degree of commitment to the working hypothesis that dreams, like all other mental phenomena, must be explained in terms of the natural minds of the persons who experience them. . . . [U]nless we are to take the "miracle" hypothesis literally, unless, that is, we are going to accept some supernatural explanation of dreams, we *must* be assigned sole responsibility even for the most "delicate" of our dream scenarios. It can be no other way. We appropriately may stand in awe of the generativity of the sleeping mind which creates such dreams. But we must go beyond awe to understanding. (1978b, 3–4)

Foulkes not only insists that dreaming can be exhaustively explained as a product of the "natural powers of the mind," he argues that dreaming is generated by the same cognitive systems that produce the ordinary speech of waking life. Dreams do not speak in a "special language"; they speak in the same basic language, following the same basic grammatical rules, that we use when we are awake.

The study on children's dreams that Foulkes conducted over a five-year period at the University of Wyoming demonstrated both the ordinariness of dreaming and its dependence on general cognitive and linguistic development. The study involved two groups of children (one starting at ages 3–4, the other starting at ages 9–10) who slept in the laboratory for nine non-consecutive nights every other year. A total of 46 children participated, and Foulkes made 2,711 awakenings during the five years. His basic findings were that children's dreams become longer, more active, and more complex as the children grow up. The three- to five-year olds in his study recalled the fewest dreams, and those dreams they did report were very short and static. Usually, these younger children did not appear as characters in their own dreams, or they appeared only as passive observers. Animal figures were remarkably common in these children's dreams. The reports of the five- to six-year olds gradually became more "dreamlike" in terms of action, theme, and narrative complexity. The seven- to eight-year olds had dreams with still greater degrees of dynamism and symbolic sophistication. By early adolescence the dreams were regularly including characters and themes from the broader social world (school, peer groups, etc.) and had become comparable to adult dreams in terms of length and structure.

Foulkes concludes that contrary to popular stereotypes, children's dreams are not filled with overwhelming anxieties, nor with simple wish fulfillments, nor with profound archetypal symbolism. Rather, children's dreams are quite ordinary expressions of how their developing minds are processing daily life experiences: "the most common plot sequences in the child's dream involve everyday forms of social interaction, with a particularly strong emphasis on play activity. Plot resolutions in dreams tend to be realistic and appropriate, rather than grandiosely self-serving" (1979, 148). Children's dreams are thus powerful evidence that dreaming is a cognitive process that develops in complexity, sophistication, and power along with other cognitive processes.

In his studies of adult dreaming Foulkes challenges another common belief: dreams are not wild, random, utterly bizarre creations, but are in fact quite orderly, coherent, and well-structured. Dream reports gathered from people sleeping in the laboratory indicate that the vast majority of dreams obey the same basic rules of logical association that govern our waking thought and language. While Foulkes grants that dreams do emerge out of personally relevant thoughts and emotions, he sees no proof that dreams are saying anything in particular. Unlike waking speech, dreams are not intended to communicate a specific message: "I conclude that we have no sense of intention during dreaming and we are unable, asleep or awake, to reconstruct plausibly why we dreamed a particular dream because there was no intention in the formation of any particular dream image" (Foulkes 1982b, 176–177). For Foulkes, as for Freud, the essence of dreaming is set of cognitive mechanisms by which thought and language are structured—"that is, mechanisms whose investment is not so much in saying any particular thing as in insuring that whatever is said is literally and thematically comprehensible" (1982b, 186).

Foulkes's basic argument is that the sleeping mind is not functionally distinct from the waking mind. The human mind is always operating as an information-processing system, he says, whether it is producing waking thoughts during the day or dreams during the night.

While he is skeptical about any effort to interpret special meanings hidden in dream contents, Foulkes affirms that dreaming probably does serve a number of valuable psychological functions:

- The complex stories and plots found in dreams suggests that dreaming allows people to exercise their powers of narrative integration, making symbolic knowledge more easily accessible to waking consciousness: "Becoming human is, from this perspective, learning to understand and to be able to tell 'stories.' Dreaming surely might play some role in this process" (1985, 202).
- The complex forms of sensory imagery created by the dreaming mind indicates that dreaming helps promote "the multimodal representation and integration of symbolic knowledge" (1985, 202).

- The appearance in dreams of memories from the recent past and from the distant past makes it likely that dreaming contributes to our conscious ability to retrieve and integrate various kinds of memory.
- The strange, "unreal" qualities of dreams "permits an enhancement of the range of 'world' experiences to which our minds are exposed. On the one hand, this could help to program our minds to deal with novel situations adaptively. On the other hand, the very unreality of dreams could contribute to the development of what Freud called 'reality testing'" (1985, 202).
- The various forms of conscious thought and self-reflection experienced while dreaming "may contribute to the development and elaboration of a distinctively human self-consciousness. What we know about dreaming in early childhood is at least consistent with this possibility" (1985, 203).

HARRY HUNT AND THE MULTIPLICITY OF DREAMS

Foulkes's strictly grammatical, anti-intentional approach to the cognitive psychology of dreams has generated a number of spirited rebuttals. The most sophisticated of these responses to Foulkes comes from Harry Hunt, a psychologist at Brock University in St. Catherines, Ontario.

In *The Multiplicity of Dreams* (1989) Hunt argues that cognitive psychology must draw upon the observations and findings of other academic fields (e.g., anthropology, history of religions, literary criticism) if it wants to develop a truly comprehensive model of dream formation and function. While Foulkes insists that only dream reports gathered from the sleep laboratory are valid evidence, Hunt replies that the more unusual types of dreams reported outside the sleep lab can offer special insights into the potentialities of the dreaming process. He says, "laboratory dreams are generally fairly boring, while it is precisely the more infrequent variations that call attention to dreams in the first place and make them uniquely worthy of study" (1989, 92). Dreams must be studied in their natural setting if we are to understand their true characteristics and functions.

After examining the full spectrum of different types of dreams, the common *and* the rare, Hunt offers the following classification:

- *Personal-mnemonic dreams*: relating to ordinary, daily matters in the dreamer's personal life.
- *Medical-somatic dreams*: relating to physiological processes of the dreamer's body; these dreams occur frequently during an illness or following an accident.
- *Prophetic dreams*: presenting omens or images of the future that may come true.
- *Archetypal-spiritual dreams*: involving vivid, powerful encounters with seemingly transcendent forces; these dreams often also include extremely strong physical or "titanic" sensations.
- *Nightmares*: involving terrifying, deeply upsetting images, themes, and emotions.
- *Lucid dreams*: involving a consciousness within the dream that the individual is dreaming.

Hunt says that these different types of dreams do not occur with equal frequency. On the contrary, some of them occur very rarely. But it is vitally important, he says, that we recognize the genuine existence of *all* these different types:

We find in each historical era and phase of culture a shift in relative importance across a common spectrum of dream typologies. But despite these shifts in the predominant definition and theory of dreaming, despite the contrasting ontological assumptions of these cultures, there is evidence that the same forms of dream experience continue to recur. . . . [T]here is a natural order of dream forms. (90)

Hunt challenges all dream theories that are based solely on the characteristics of only one of these dream forms (for instance, he says that Foulkes and Freud considered only dreams of the personal-mnemonic type in developing their theories). Hunt's goal is to develop a cognitive psychological understanding that can account for the processes that generate all the different types of dreams, that can give us "insight into a deeper unity of dream formation" (74).

The chief task, as Hunt sees it, is to reconcile two opposing approaches to the question of how dreams are formed. According to one general theory, held by Foulkes, Freud, Hobson, and several cognitive psychologists, dreaming involves a battle between forces of mental *chaos* and forces of mental *order*. The partly-random, partly-organized imagery of our dreams results from an uneasy compromise between these two warring forces. The research focus here is on the constructive activities of the forces of mental order: how exactly are the chaotic images and memories thrown up by REM sleep and/or the unconscious cognitively transformed into the partially organized products of our dreams? Freud describes the four mechanisms of the dream-work, Hobson speaks of the "synthesis" side of activation-synthesis, and Foulkes refers to the grammatical structures governing ordinary speech. In each of these theories, dreams are explained as the products of higher level mental processes that impose order on the disruptive lower level mental inputs.

Hunt says the other general approach to dream formation, best expressed by Jung and by James Hillman (a prominent Jungian analyst), asserts that the seemingly disruptive forces in dreams are actually the spontaneous expressions of a powerful symbolic intelligence which is different from but not inferior to waking rational thought. Here, the research focus is on the incredibly bizarre, fantastic images that fill so many dreams: what can waking consciousness learn from these mysteriously creative dream images whose beauty rivals great works of art and whose wisdom compares to the sacred teachings of the world's religions? Both Jung and Hillman insist that the symbolic imagery of dreaming can bring forth profound meanings and powerful healing energies—if waking consciousness can surrender its inflated self-image and enter into a true dialogue with the unconscious.

The bitter disagreements between these two basic approaches to dreams are unnecessary, Hunt says, because both approaches are right about different types of dreams. Foulkes, Hobson, and Freud are right that cognitively-sophisticated narrative and grammatical processes are primary in the shaping of many dreams (i.e., personal-mnemonic dreams). But Jung and Hillman are also right that spontaneous, highly creative visual-spatial imagery often appears in dreams and takes the lead in forming the rarer "intensified" types of dreams. Hunt argues that in most cases both cognitive modes, the narrative-grammatical and the visual-spatial, are working together, combining and interacting in many different ways to form the many different types of dreaming experience: "We arrive then at a picture of two systems, both self-referential and creatively recombinatory expressions of the human symbolic capacity, interacting in different measures to produce both normative dreaming and its imagistically predominant variations" (168).

Hunt offers one of his own dreams (which occurred while he was in the process of separating from his wife) to illustrate how strange, unexpected visual-spatial elements do not necessarily disrupt the grammatical structure and thematic continuity of a dream but may actually enhance the dream's dramatic sense, fulfilling and completing its narrative intention.

I am traveling with my wife and children, looking for a parking place in order to visit the Tibetan National Museum. The only parking areas I can find are in highway rest areas and I realize that unless I hurry the museum will close. Accordingly, I now drive directly to the museum (a huge building with multiple wings and four or five floors). Leaving my car and family in front, I run inside. I enter a massive foyer and find to my intense disappointment that the museum has just closed.

Looking about, I notice an open door to a small room off to one side. Entering, I find myself in the private apartment of an older, very thin women [sic], who is apparently the museum caretaker. The room is primitive and archaic. The women [sic] is in one corner steadily stirring a very large pot of boiling water. As I approach more closely I see in the pot a carved wooden manikin about two feet tall. As the woman stirs, ignoring me, the room is filled with an eerie, high-pitched wailing sound. I realize with growing horror that the sound emanates from the wooden manikin, which is becoming progressively more lifelike as she stirs—its scream of pain becomes more and more shrill and frenzied and then begins to turn into an uncanny and strangely beautiful song. I realize that the price of the vivification of the manikin is the terrible agony that produces this song, and I awaken in a cold sweat. (166)[2]

Hunt points to the sharp discontinuity in this dream between the initial scene of driving around with his family in search of a parking place and the final scene of hearing the little manikin's agonized scream turned into beautiful song. Foulkes would likely see such a radical shift in both character and setting as another instance of the random, meaningless disruptions so common in dreams. But Hunt argues that the two scenes in fact combine to enhance the overall dramatic power of the dream. The first scene establishes a contrast between his family responsibilities and his personal interests in Tibetan culture, a contrast that seems to have symbolic relations to his impending marital separation. The second scene develops that contrast further, expanding it into a symbolic polarity of dying and coming alive, "with the further implication that such a coming alive will be mediated by the feminine and, of course, by immense pain" (167). In this case, then, the apparent narrative discontinuity and bizarreness actually helped "to weld this dream together as a single dramatic whole. . . . [It] constitutes a powerful metaphor for a major dilemma and an acute anticipation of its resolution" (167).

Hunt's experimental research indicates that there are a number of relatively distinct types of dreaming. Each of these different dream types is formed by a different combination of cognitive processes, and each dream type has its own line of potential development. Hunt admits that the "multiplicity of dreams" makes scientific research quite difficult, because investigators must be sensitive to the overlap and interplay of all the various dream types. Furthermore, investigators must take into account the many factors (physiological, psychological, and cultural) that promote the experience of some dream types and inhibit the experience of other types. In modern Western culture, for example, personal-mnemonic dreams are considered normal, while reports of medical-somatic and prophetic dreams are often greeted with disbelief and ridicule. Hunt believes these cultural attitudes have a subtle but powerful impact on the development of the cognitive processes involved in dreaming.

For this reason, Hunt is skeptical about absolutist claims regarding the function of dreaming: "there may not be a fundamental *function* of dreaming, any more than we can find a function for human existence generally. . . . It may be because dreaming has no fixed function that it is open to so many different uses" (76).

ERNEST HARTMANN ON NIGHTMARES AND THE BOUNDARIES OF THE MIND

Ernest Hartmann is a psychiatrist who teaches at Tufts University and directs the Sleep Research Laboratory at Lemuel Shattuck Hospital in Boston. Among his many books are *The Biology of Dreaming* (1967), *Sleep and Dreaming* (1970), and *The Functions of Sleep* (1973). In 1984 he published *The Nightmare: The Psychology and Biology of Terrifying Dreams*, in which he combines clinical and experimental studies to examine the question of who has nightmares, and why they have them. In formulating his answer, Hartmann develops the notion of "boundaries of the mind": frequent nightmare sufferers have "thin" psychological boundaries, thus making them more vulnerable to anxiety-filled dreams (Hartmann gives a more detailed account of this notion in his 1991 book *Boundaries of the Mind*).

Hartmann says that sleep laboratory research has indicated that there are two very different frightening dream phenomena: the nightmare and the night terror. He offers as an example of a night terror the following sleep lab report:

Fifty minutes after sleep onset during stage 4 sleep, a body movement occurs, HS [the subject] rolls over screaming repeatedly, 'Help, help.' He mutters about swallowing something and choking. His pulse rate has increased from 60 to 90 per minute during the 15 seconds it takes him to awaken. He quickly falls asleep again, and later has no recall for the event. (1984, 11)

As an example of a nightmare, Hartmann recounts this experience of a woman awakened in his sleep lab at 7:50 a.m., after a nineteen-minute REM period:

I was at my parents' house and they had gone out to some party . . . or something like that and I was home alone. Suddenly, this guy from next door came over and he just kind of walked through the house. And I asked him what he needed and he told me he was having trouble moving his house. And it turned out that he was having some kind of legal trouble so that he had to move his house a certain number of feet. And in the dream I went out into the yard and he had moved his whole house and it crashed into my parents' house. . . . I got really scared and I started to run. And this other guy ran after me and caught me . . . and I kept struggling. (14)

Hartmann explains that night terrors occur during stage 3 or 4 NREM sleep, usually within the first two hours following sleep onset. They involve sudden arousal, screaming, sweating, and troubles with breathing. There is little or no imagery associated with the experience, and the person often does not recall it when fully awakened. Night terrors are not, strictly speaking, dreams at all. Hartmann says they are better understood as "disorders of arousal" (20). Nightmares, however, are very different experiences from night terrors. Hartmann says nightmares tend to be long, frightening dreams occurring during REM sleep, most often during the later parts of the night, that awaken the person with their vivid, clearly remembered imagery.

A third category of frightening dream, different from both nightmares and night terrors, is the post-traumatic nightmare. These frightening dreams are provoked by a terrible waking-life experience (e.g., being in wartime combat, having an auto accident, being physically or sexually assaulted). The waking-life experience is then replayed in frighteningly direct, graphic detail in the person's dreams, over and over again. In some cases the nightmares continue to plague the person decades after the original traumatic experience. However, Hartmann says that with most post-traumatic nightmares the repetitions fade rapidly, especially if the person is able to talk about the experience and make some progress in integrating it into the rest of his or her life:

A typical story here is [that] after a traumatic event, the event may be dreamt almost literally a few times and then gradually other elements are included as the event becomes woven into the rest of one's dream life—'I was with some friends at this place we used to have near New York. Some kind of party; and then those guys came in who looked like the guys who attacked me last month, except in the dream they were wearing these funny old-fashioned suits. I was kind of scared, but I kept talking to my girlfriend, and ignored them. (192)

Post-traumatic nightmares may occur during any stage of sleep, indicating that they are "a third psychophysiological entity, not identical to either ordinary nightmares or night terrors" (188).

To explain why some people frequently suffer from long, terrifying dreams, Hartmann uses the notion of "boundaries of the mind." The natural development of mental structures that begins in childhood involves learning to distinguish between self and other, inside and outside, fantasy and reality, and other basic features of life; and each of these distinctions implies psychological realms with boundaries around them. Using data from both clinical and experimental research, Hartmann argues that frequent nightmare sufferers have "thin or permeable boundaries":

They may form less firm ego boundaries, less solid boundaries around their feeling of self, and less firm interpersonal boundaries among others. These people are painfully sensitive to, and in danger from, their own wishes and impulses as well as demands or threats from the world outside. Indeed, the childhood histories obtained from the nightmare sufferers are those of persons who were always unusually sensitive, unusually open and vulnerable, and thus to some extent felt different from others. They often have had a painful and sometimes lonely childhood followed by a stormy and difficult adolescence. As they became adults, some of them—and this is more true of women—were able to maintain the openness inherent in a thin-boundary condition and were able to apply it in their work as artists, teachers, or therapists, but it was a difficult state to maintain and they were sometimes vulnerable to psychosis and also to physical injury. (158)

In contrast to people with "thick boundaries," who have stronger defenses against threats from the outer world and from unconscious fears and impulses, people with thin boundaries are more easily overwhelmed by both externally and internally generated threats—resulting in a greater vulnerability to frequent nightmares.

Occasional nightmares are normal for all people, those with thin as well as thick boundaries. Young children have the most nightmares of any age group (and young children are also especially prone to experience night terrors). Hartmann estimates that the average incidence of nightmares among adults is one to two per year. Certain factors tend to increase nightmare frequency: some medications (especialy L-dopa, used in the treatment of Parkinson's disease), physical or mental illnesses, and in general any kind of major life stress or trauma. Hartmann says that for all people, "nightmares appear to be especially frequent in situations that involve helplessness or that remind a person of childhood feelings of helplessness" (36).

Hartmann's research has pointed to some important connections between thin psychological boundaries and dreaming. People who have thin boundaries (as determined by their scores on a battery of psychological tests) remember far more dreams than do those people who have thick boundaries. Furthermore, people with thin boundaries have dreams that are more vivid, detailed, and emotional than are the dreams of people with thick boundaries. Hartmann has argued that dreaming itself can be considered a thin boundary state, characterized by openness, fluidity, and ambiguity. In his view the basic nature of dreaming is that it makes psychological connections more broadly than does waking thought; these connections are not the products of a random process, but are guided by the dominant emotional concerns of the dreamer.

FACTORS INFLUENCING DREAM RECALL: EXPERIMENTAL STUDIES

The question of why people remember some of their dreams and not others has puzzled almost every modern dream psychologist. Freud, for example, said dreams are never intended to be remembered because of the deceptive workings of the censor, so it should be no surprise that people rarely recall their dreams. Jung replied that poor dream recall is due not to any internal censor, but rather to the inability of rational waking consciousness to understand the special symbolic images and themes so often expressed in dreams.

As with so much in the modern psychology of dreaming, the findings of sleep laboratory research cast an entirely new light on this question. According to psychologist Kathryn Belicki (whose research guides much of the following discussion), when subjects sleeping in the laboratory are awakened during a REM period, they recall a dream approximately 80 percent of the time, or 4–5 dreams per night (Belicki 1987, 187). However, these same people recall on average only 2–3 dreams per week when sleeping normally at home. These findings have greatly added to the mystery surrounding the question of dream recall: it now seems that everyone is dreaming a number of times each night, and yet forgetting the vast majority of their dream experiences.

Experimental psychologists who study the nature of memory have suggested that one major impediment to dream recall is the general difficulty of retrieving from memory storage any experience that occurs during sleep (Belicki 1987, 187). But, as Belicki notes, this still leaves open the question of why people occasionally do remember their dreams. It also leaves open the question of why certain people tend to remember lots of their dreams, while other people virtually never remember their dreams.

Research indicates that four different factors influence the daily variations in each individual's dream recall (Belicki 1987, 188–191). First is the condition under which people are awakened from sleep. If people are immediately distracted when they wake up (e.g., by an alarm clock, by other people, by pressing concerns about school or work), they are much less likely to recall their dreams than if they wake up in a slow, quiet, and unhurried fashion. Second is motivation. People recall many more dreams when they have some special interest in the subject, perhaps because they are taking a psychology class, or they are reading a book on dreams, or they are seeing a psychotherapist. Third is the characteristics of particular dream experiences. Dreams that occur toward the end of the night seem to be more easily recalled the next morning than dreams that occur earlier in the sleep cycle; and longer, more intense dreams seem to be remembered better than shorter, less intense dreams. The fourth factor is life stress. In many cases, dream recall increases during times of stress and crisis (e.g., a divorce, an illness, a natural disaster). The effect of life stress on dream recall seems especially strong among women.

Turning to the question of why some people are "high" dream recallers while others are "low" recallers, one widespread theory is that people who have a generally defensive personality tend to remember fewer of their dreams. Another theory holds that people who possess more developed powers of imagination, whose cognitive style involves a greater ability to use imagery and creative processes while awake, tend to remember more of their dreams. But Belicki says both of these theories should be regarded with caution:

[A] major problem that exists with all the research on personality and ability factors is that the observed relationships tend to be disappointingly small. One possible reason for this state of affairs is that it has been widely assumed that differences among people in dream recall are stable differences, consistent over time. However, in my early research when I regularly asked subjects to estimate their typical weekly dream recall, many individuals would insist they did not have a typical amount of recall, that their recall fluctuated dramatically from one time period to the next. (197–198)

Perhaps the most important point to take from this research is that any psychological theory attempting to explain the function of dreaming must account for these enduring questions about dream recall. Specifically, it must account for the facts that (1) most people regularly forget almost all of their dream experiences, and (2) some people naturally remember one or two dreams every night ("high" recallers), while other people never remember any of their dreams, under any circumstances ("low" recallers).

EXPERIMENTAL PSYCHOLOGY'S ANSWERS TO THE THREE BASIC QUESTIONS

Formation

Experimental psychologists generally agree that what we experience as dreams are constructed and shaped by the same basic mental operations that are at work in our conscious waking thought. For Piaget, dreaming is best understood in terms of the fundamental psychological tendencies toward accommodation and assimilation. Hall emphasizes the continuity between dream content and waking-life thoughts and behaviors. Foulkes focuses on the identities in dreaming and waking thought processes, particularly language formation. Hunt discusses the role in dreams of both narrative-grammatical and visual-spatial cognitive processes. Hartmann speaks of boundaries of the mind which structure waking and dreaming experiences. Experimental psychologists also agree that as these basic mental operations develop from childhood into adulthood, so does dreaming: the dreams of adults are more complex and sophisticated than are the dreams of children.

Functions

Most experimental psychologists grant that dreaming plays some important role in the mind's ongoing effort to process both external and internal information. Thus, dreaming serves to promote the general adaptation of people to their environment, helping them to organize their perceptions, to exercise their cognitive powers, and to connect and integrate new experiences with past memories. Some experimental psychologists (e.g., Hunt) argue that dreaming may also provide people with stunningly original metaphors which speak directly to their major waking-life concerns.

Interpretation

Experimental psychologists like Foulkes are skeptical regarding attempts to interpret what particular dreams might mean. Others, however, are more willing to use their research to guide efforts at dream interpretation. Hall stresses the importance of interpreting whole series of dreams; knowing the basic features of the whole series can be of great help in determining what any single dream in the series might mean. For Hunt, the existence of multiple types of dreams requires interpreters to be careful not to misapply models appropriate for understanding one type of dream in trying to understand a different type of dream. Most experimental psychologists offer their research not as an interpretive system in itself but as a source of valuable empirical information about dreams and dreaming from which anyone involved in the practice of dream interpretation can benefit.

NOTES

1. Piaget has grave reservations about Jung, however. He comments, "Jung has an amazing capacity for construction, but a certain contempt for logical and rational activity, which he has contracted through daily contact with mythological and symbolic thought, has made him inclined to be content with too little in the way of proof. The better to understand the realities of which he speaks, he adopts an anti-rationalist attitude, and the surprising comparisons of which he has the secret cannot fail sometimes to disturb the critical reader" (1962, 196).

2. The first two misspellings of "women" are in Hunt's original text.

Chapter 7

Popular Psychology: Bringing Dreams to the Masses

"I have a dream . . ."

Martin Luther King, Jr., speech given at the
Lincoln Memorial, August 28, 1963

Historical surveys of modern psychological dream research often neglect to mention the contributions of psychologists whose work focuses primarily on teaching basic principles of psychology and mental health to the general public. This is unfortunate, because these "pop" psychologists have genuinely advanced psychological knowledge of dreams by exploring the dream lives of ordinary people, outside the limited and often artificial contexts of the psychotherapy office and the sleep laboratory. Today's popular psychologists are carrying on the tradition of Artemidorus, the Greek dream interpreter who almost two thousand years ago made a careful, respectful study of the dream lives of ordinary people.

A number of currents came together in North America and western Europe in the 1960s and early 1970s to form a broad-based popular psychological approach to dreaming. By this time the teachings of Freud and Jung had been disseminated widely enough that their basic ideas about dreams, symbols, and the unconscious were familiar to a significant percentage of the population. The discoveries of the sleep lab had been broadly publicized by newspapers and magazines, and these media reports put special emphasis on the finding that *all* humans have regular amounts of REM sleep, indicating that *all* humans dream every night. The counterculture movement of the 1960s had renewed people's interest in altered states of consciousness, which could be experienced through dreams as well as through drugs, music, and meditation. And reports from anthropologists about the dream practices of non-Western cultures (e.g., Native Americans, Australian aborigines, African tribespeople) began reaching popular audiences, describing how people in these cultures cherish their dreams as powerful wellsprings of spiritual wisdom, artistic creativity, and guidance in both personal and communal life.

A group of psychologists took these different sources of information about dreams and, with the help of newly-developed techniques of mass market communication, addressed the practical interests and concerns of ordinary people. This chapter describes the major works of the leading popular psychologists, and discusses their contributions to modern dream psychology.

SELF-HELP BOOKS ON DREAMS: ANN FARADAY, PATRICIA GAR-FIELD, AND GAYLE DELANEY

The current wave of popular interest in dreams was generated in large part by the work of three psychologists: Ann Faraday, Patricia Garfield, and Gayle Delaney. All three wrote highly successful mass-market books on dreams that aimed at giving general readers simple, practical, "how-to" suggestions for understanding their dreams.

Faraday's *Dream Power* (1972) begins with one of her own childhood dreams:

When I was a small child, I used to have recurring dreams of being pursued by 'Creamers'—men wearing long white coats and tall white hats—whose leader was named Beasley. I remember asking my mother what Creamers were, and she replied, "I think they're chocolates, darling." But I knew they weren't—they were men dressed in white who chased me throughout the night. (1972, 13)

Faraday's interest in dreams remained strong, and she eventually did graduate research in a sleep laboratory on frequency of dream recall. But her research disappointed her—"I learned much about rats, reaction time, and statistics, but nothing about myself" (1972, 14). Then, after a "totally frustrating experience of Freudian analysis which did violence both to me and to my dreams by trying to fit us into a rigid, limited, and dogmatic theory" (1974, xiii) and after an experience of Jungian analysis that was only slightly less negative, Faraday decided to develop her own approach to dreaming and dream interpretation. *Dream Power* was the result.

The book outlines Faraday's approach to "the use of dreams at home," which she calls "The Three Faces of Dreaming." According to this approach, dreams should always be looked at in three different ways:

Looking outward, they [dreams] often bring to our attention things we have failed to notice in waking life. Second, we may use them as mirrors that reflect our attitudes and prejudices, and finally, by looking inward and treating the dream as an existential message about the state of our inner world, we can often discover the hidden source of our problems and regain long-buried aspects of the personality. (1972, 16)

In the final section of *Dream Power* Faraday looks forward to what the use of dreams for greater self-knowledge could mean for families, churches, schools, business, politics, and society as a whole—"I believe this last part of the twentieth century is likely to be marked by all kinds of experiments in new ways of promoting self-understanding and emotional growth, and I am sure that the use of dreams has an enormous part to play in this" (1972, 269). She also discusses the potential of dreams to provide creative inspirtation, to reveal profound spiritual truths, and to open the door to ecstatic, transcendental experiences similar to other altered states of consciousness.

The Dream Game (1974) offers a more detailed set of practical instructions to help people understand their dreams better. Faraday describes how to keep a dream diary, how to interpret common dream themes (e.g., dreams of falling, flying, nudity, examinations, losing teeth, losing money or valuables, finding money or valuables, and sex), and how to ask help from dreams through the practice of *dream incubation* (going to sleep with a specific question in mind, and then interpreting that night's dream as a response to the question). Faraday chose the title *The Dream Game* for this book to emphasize her eclectic, playful approach to the various ways of interpreting dreams. For example, she shows her readers how to play the "Freudian game" of looking for sexual symbols, and how to play the "Jungian game" of looking for archetypal symbols. Faraday's own preference is for the "Gestalt game" of looking for topdog-underdog symbols and conflicts, and she devotes much of her book to recounting lively, insight-rich Gestalt dialogues between dreamers and different characters from their dreams. But as helpful as all these various dream games may be, Faraday insists that "none of these, nor any other way of working with dreams, is universally true; and we do violence to our dreams if we try to force them into restricting theories" (1974, xvii).

Patricia Garfield's *Creative Dreaming* (1974) is aimed at helping people plan and control their dreams so they can unify their personalities, deal better with waking-life fears and problems, and become more creative in all they do. Garfield first started keeping a dream diary when she was fourteen, and she says that throughout her graduate studies in clinical psychology, her marriage, her parenting, her divorce, and her second marriage, "I found that my dreams were a source of self-reflection and understanding. They helped support me through difficult times" (1988, xi). She wrote *Creative Dreaming* to share her experiences and insights with others:

The prevailing idea [at this time] was that dreams are experiences occurring during sleep that only afterwards may be analyzed and worked with by professionals. Dreams were out of the province of the average dreamer; it was said that they could not be influenced by the dreamer and that dream style changed little over a lifetime. I knew this was not true. Working with my own dreams since my teenage years had taught me much about myself.

Each dreamer, I believed, could benefit from understanding his or her own dreams. (1988, xii)

Creative Dreaming differs from Faraday's two books in that it draws more heavily on historical and cross-cultural sources. Garfield provides lengthy narrative accounts of the dream practices of ancient Greeks, Native Americans, Malaysian tribespeople, and Tibetan Buddhists. She says that in many of these cultures people developed the ability to become conscious *within* their dreams, and thus to control what happens in their dream worlds. This wonderful ability allows people to fearlessly approach whatever threatens them in their dreams, transforming fear and weakness into power and strength. Garfield says that such exhilarating experiences of dream control and creativity "produce a mood of capability that carries over into waking life, providing a foundation for confident, capable action" (1974, 14).

Synthesizing the teachings of these many different cultures, Garfield says that anyone can learn to become a creative dreamer. The crucial starting point is to take dreams seriously and to recognize that becoming conscious within a dream is indeed possible:

In every system we have reviewed, the dreamer's attitude is of prime importance. Creative dreaming is rather like believing in the possibility of love; if you have never experienced it, it is difficult to believe it can exist for you. Once love has become a reality for you, no cynic on earth can persuade you that it does not exist. So it is with creative dreaming. Once you have been fully conscious during a dream, you *know* it can be done. (1974, 199)

Garfield goes on to give detailed instructions on how to develop consciousness within the dream state. She says people should go to sleep in a quiet, peaceful condition, and should focus their pre-sleep attention on the specific goal of becoming aware within their dreams. It may take a great deal of time and practice, but she says that eventually the experience of creative dreaming can come to anyone.

Gayle Delaney's *Living Your Dreams* (1979) explains the nature of dreaming by means of a film metaphor: dreams are "movies of the mind" in which the individual dreamer is the producer, the screenwriter, the director, and the star of each dream (xi, 5–7). Delaney opens her book with a dream she experienced after several years in Jungian analysis:

It was a beautiful night. The stars glittered excitingly in a navy blue satin sky. Oh, those stars! They twinkled with the spirit of an Irish Setter wagging his tail with joy at the return of his master. Here I was, in Hollywood. I felt welcome and happy and full of expectations that something good was about to happen.

The next thing I knew, I was being led into the spectacular home of Otto Preminger [a producer and director of several Hollywood films in the 1940s and 1950s]. I had never seen it before. Now, as I sat in the main living room, I savored its beauty. The room was decorated in the best Art Deco style. There were circular mirrors, palm trees, and blue silks covering great furniture forms. Everything was designed with symmetry and yet surprise. I was surrounded by luxurious and brilliant design reminiscent of some Fred Astaire and Ginger Rogers movie set.

I awaited the entrance of the great movie producer. What would he say to me? Why was I invited to come here? Would he say, 'I want to make you a star'? Would I be able at last to ice skate and dance my heart out in the movies? I kept waiting for Mr. Preminger to walk into the room. I waited, and waited, . . . and waited.

Slowly, slowly, I began to realize that this marvelous house belonged to me! Somehow Otto Preminger's house was mine! (1979, 4)

Delaney says this dream helped her stop looking at her dreams as something she received from the outside, and start experiencing them as her own creations. To her, Otto Preminger was the greatest movie producer of all time, so his house turning out to be her house meant that she was the "Otto Preminger" of her own dream productions.

With this as her starting point, Delaney devotes her book to describing techniques to help people be more effective in directing their dream productions and more successful in understanding the messages conveyed by their private cinematic creations. After presenting basic techniques on keeping a dream diary and practicing dream incubation (she calls her method "phrase focusing or secular dream incubation" [20]), Delaney outlines her "dream interview" approach to interpreting dreams.

She says the best way to begin grasping the meaning of a dream is to ask the dreamer simply to describe and define the dream's imagery. Delaney says "you may find the producer more willing to answer your questions if you first ask him to pretend that you come from another planet" (52); in this way, the dreamer is encouraged to become aware of the special ideas, beliefs, and associations he or she has in relation to a particular dream image. For example, if a person dreams of a dog, the interviewer would say, "Pretend I'm from another planet, and don't know what a dog is. Can you describe a 'dog' to me?" The dreamer might say a dog has four legs, has a good sense of smell, makes a barking sound, is very faithful—and then the dreamer might suddenly realize that the dog in the dream symbolizes a waking-life problem having to do with faithfulness.

The goal of the dream interview method is to help the dreamer discover the connections or bridges between the dream and waking life. Delaney emphasizes that "it is appallingly easy to misinterpret another's dream," and she warns interviewers to be careful about forcing their interpretations onto the dreamer (53). She encourages people to practice her methods, to see how easy it can be to interpret dreams: "most dreams will yield their messages to a skillful interviewer with surprisingly little effort" (56).

These self-help books by Faraday, Garfield, and Delaney have sold hundreds of thousands of copies worldwide, aided in large part by the authors' skills in communicating their basic ideas through television, radio, magazines, and other mass media outlets. The commercial success of their books has given a tremendous boost to the general public's interest in modern dream psychology. Their books have also given other dream researchers a great deal of food for thought. Faraday, Garfield, and Delaney have shown that people who are not in formal psychotherapy can learn and fruitfully apply simple principles of dream interpretation. They have shown that dreams can give people valuable insights to help deal with common waking-life problems (e.g., troubles with family members, with work, with health). And, they have shown that becoming more aware of dreams can enhance people's self-esteem, creativity, and spiritual vitality.

DREAM SHARING GROUPS: MONTAGUE ULLMAN AND JEREMY TAYLOR

Although Faraday, Garfield, and Delaney all discuss the sharing of dreams in group settings, the practice has been most fully developed by Montague Ullman and Jeremy Taylor.

Ullman is a psychoanalytically-trained psychiatrist who founded the Dream Laboratory at the Maimonides Medical Center in New York. In the 1960s his work in community psychiatry led him to consider various ways in which psychiatric services could be brought to communities where such services were unavailable. Then, in the 1970s, Ullman went to Sweden to help develop a psychoanalytic training program and to do further work in community mental health. In both countries Ullman focused his efforts on teaching people his methods of group "dream appreciation" (Ullman and Zimmerman 1979, 12). In Sweden he has actually received government sponsorship and funding to support community dream-sharing groups. Ullman says his basic approach to working with dreams in group settings derives from two basic facts about dreams:

First, it is useful to have support as we struggle to bring an honest perspective to our dreams. Second, others who are not personally involved in the dream can often 'read' our metaphors better than we can, simply because they do not have to deal with the consequences of their reading. (Ullman and Zimmerman 1979, 13)

In his book *Working With Dreams* (1979), co-authored with Nan Zimmerman, Ullman lays out a five-stage process for working with dreams in groups. In the first stage, the dreamer shares the dream with the group. In the second, the group reflects on the feelings, images, and metaphors they perceive and empathize with in the dream. During this stage the dreamer remains silent, and simply listens while the group responds to the dream. Ullman emphasizes that all the responses are useful, even the "wrong" ones, because "a 'wrong' response helps a dreamer define what the image is not and thereby may help the dreamer get closer to defining what it is" (217). After the group has considered every detail of the dream, the dreamer is invited in the third stage to respond to the group's responses. A dialogue between the group and the dreamer ensues in the fourth stage, and the fifth and final stage has the dreamer reflecting alone on all the meanings that have come up during the group process. Ullman says,

If the group members have been successful they have functioned as midwives; they have brought the dream out to public view and helped establish the dreamer's connection to it. When this happens their job is finished and the job of the one who gave birth to the dream begins in earnest. (220)

Jeremy Taylor, a Unitarian Universalist minister, did his first formal group dream sharing while he was leading a consciousness-raising seminar on racism (as part of his alternative civilian service as a conscientious objector to the Vietnam war). As Taylor describes it in *Dream Work* (1983), when he suggested that the seminar members share and discuss their dreams in which black people appeared,

the energy for growth and transformation of personality and unconscious attitudes and fears that were released by this work was truly astonishing, even to me. The dream work was effective in bringing deep-seated unconscious ambivalences to light, and the work was further effective in transforming them, because each of us was forced to 'own' both the negative and positive images of black people in our dreams as representations of aspects of our own personalities. (16)

Taylor says the tremendous value of group dream sharing derives from the fact that by hearing the comments and reflections of a variety of different people the dreamer is "exposed to a fuller range of the dream's possible meaning" (76). Because every dream has more than one meaning, a dream-sharing group provides excellent opportunities for exploring those multiple meanings, more than can usually be discovered by working on dreams alone or with only one other person.

While dream-sharing groups can take many different forms, Taylor recommends the following structures and principles to guide any group:

- The group (ideally 6–12 people) gathers in a quiet, comfortable place.
- One of the people serves as leader or facilitator for the group, monitoring the flow of discussion and watching the time.
- After an initial "touch-in" to discuss how everyone is doing, each person in the group gets to describe one of his or her dreams.
- The group chooses one person's dream to discuss in detail, and proceeds to offer comments, ask questions, and suggest meanings regarding that dream.
- This discussion can take from fifteen minutes to two hours; usually, an effort it made to discuss more than one dream at a given meeting.
- Over the course of a few meetings, everyone in the group participates: everyone gets to share his or her own dreams, everyone gets to comment on other people's dreams, and everyone gets to have one of their dreams discussed by the group.

Taylor says the "only reliable touchstone of dream work" is the "aha!" or "tingle" feeling people get when they realize some truth about their dreams. This means that dream interpretation requires people to pay attention "with as much of [their] whole being as possible," so these flashes of intuitive discovery can be recognized (83). However, Taylor cautions that the "aha!" test should be balanced with critical self-awareness:

One of the most important things to understand about group dream work is that the flashes and tingles and ahas you feel are always signals of truth, but that it is always a truth about *oneself*, and not necessarily a truth about the other person's dream. Thus, it is always true that what is said about someone else's dream always reflects the personality and symbol structure of the person making the comment as much as or more than it reflects anything in the dream itself. For this reason it is often useful to preface any remark with the idea, "if it were *my* dream." (Taylor 1983, 83)

Taylor says this "if it were my dream" preface helps to remind everyone in the group that the dream belongs to the dreamer, that only the dreamer knows for sure what the dream means, and that the other group members are engaged in a process of projecting their own ideas, feelings, and intuitions onto the dreamer's experience.

Suppose, for example, that a person shares a dream of driving a car too fast and realizing with fear that the brakes don't work. If a group member says that "your dream means your life is speeding out of control," the comment may come across as authoritative, confrontational, and rude. But if the group member says, "If it were *my* dream, it would mean that *my* life is speeding out of control," the comment both gives the dreamer more space to reflect on the interpretation and encourages the group member to reflect on his or her own feelings that have been brought up by the other person's dream. The "if it were *my* dream . . ." preface clearly marks the comment as the group member's personal projection—a projection which may turn out to be extremely helpful to the dreamer. Taylor notes that "even though we can do nothing but project ourselves into the understanding of other people's dreams, these projections often prove to be the source of insight for the dreamer" (83–84).

Taylor says the value of group dream sharing goes beyond giving people better insights into their dreams. As his racism seminar demonstrated, sharing dreams with other people has political and social value in helping overcome the barriers of race, age, sex, and class. By revealing one's own deepest hopes and fears, by giving insights into the deepest hopes and fears of other people, and by demonstrating how projections both hinder and enhance creative human relations, dream-sharing groups promote both personal and communal transformation: "the deep sense of community which group dream work creates continues to sustain and nurture the individual creativity and courage, without which collective change is impossible" (17).

LUCID DREAMING: STEPHEN LABERGE

Lucid dreaming is the ability to become aware *within a dream* that one is dreaming. In Western culture this ability was recognized at least as early as the time of Aristotle (see Chapter 1), was noted in passing by Freud (see Chapter 2), and was discussed at some length in the books of all the aforementioned popular psychologists. But only in the last few years have scientific researchers begun making a truly detailed and systematic study of lucid dreams. The pioneer in this field is Stephen LaBerge, whose book *Lucid Dreaming* (1985) explains his psychophysiological research on lucid dreams to a mass-market audience.

LaBerge had experienced lucid dreams from the age of five, and as he grew up he became increasingly fascinated by the phenomenon. In 1977 he first read the book *Lucid Dreams* (1968) by British parapsychologist Celia Green. Green's work further stimulated LaBerge's interest, and he began keeping a journal that after seven years contained almost nine hundred lucid dream reports. The more he studied his own lucid dream experiences, the more he wanted to try to "communicate from the lucid dream to the outside world, *while* the dream was happening" (68). He entered a doctoral program in psychophysiology at Stanford University's sleep laboratory with the express intent of using sleep lab technology to achieve his goal of scientifically proving that lucid dreams really occur.

As LaBerge pursued his research he found that despite the historical testimony of people like Aristotle and despite the contemporary reports of Celia Green, Ann Faraday, Patricia Garfield, and others, most sleep and dream researchers did not accept that lucid dreams were really dreams. In large part this resistance was due to an essentially philosophical belief that a person simply could not be asleep and conscious at the same time: to be asleep is, by definition, not to be conscious. For many mainstream dream researchers, the very concept of "lucid dreaming" seemed to be a contradiction in terms.

To refute this skeptical argument, LaBerge devised an experiment. The standard tool of measurement in a sleep lab is the EEG machine, which measures eye movements during the various stages of sleep. LaBerge says,

I knew that lucid dreamers could freely look in any direction they wished while in a lucid dream, because I had done this myself. It occurred to me that by moving my (dream) eyes in a recognizable pattern, I might be able to send a signal to the outside world when I was having a lucid dream. (68)

After a number of failed attempts, LaBerge finally succeeded in becoming lucid while dreaming in Stanford's sleep laboratory. Within his dream he opened his eyes, held his finger in front of him, and moved it in a vertical line, following it carefully with his eyes. When he awoke he and his colleagues checked the data from the EEG monitor that had been attached to LaBerge while he slept: "[W]e observed two large eye movements on the polygraph record just before I awakened from a thirteen-minute REM period. Here, finally, was objective evidence that at least one lucid dream had taken place during what was clearly REM sleep!" (70) LaBerge and others soon replicated this experiment, demonstrating that within REM sleep a person can become conscious and make prearranged eye signals through an EEG monitor to outside observers.

One important implication of LaBerge's research is that it adds further evidence to a widespread point of criticism against Hobson's activation-synthesis hypothesis of dreaming. According to Hobson's hypothesis, the "higher" mental functions of the forebrain play only a secondary role in dream formation, making partially coherent dream imagery out of random neural firings from the brainstem. But lucid dreams clearly show that higher-level mental functions can at times play a primary role in dream formation (as when, for example, a lucid dreamer purposefully decides to change one dream scene into another). Research on lucid dreaming greatly strengthens the argument that dream formation is a "two-way street" between brainstem and forebrain and not the one-directional process envisioned by Hobson.

LaBerge's book *Lucid Dreaming* moves quickly from his scientific research to more practical questions of how to apply lucid dreaming in the lives of ordinary people. First, he describes various techniques that people can use to stimulate their own lucid dream experiences, for lucid dreaming "is an ability that can be gained or improved by training" (139). (Following his graduate school research, LaBerge began work on a set of electronic goggles that could signal to a sleeping person whenever he or she entered REM sleep, thus prompting lucidity within a dream.) LaBerge then discusses the possibilities that lucid dreaming can help give people access to valuable unconscious knowledge, improve physical health by allowing greater control over physiological processes, and promote the psychological integration of ignored parts of one's personality. LaBerge says lucid dreaming may be especially helpful in treating nightmare sufferers:

This is a very important potential of lucid dreaming, since when we 'escape' from a nightmare by awakening, we have not dealt with the problem of our fear or our frightening dream, but merely relieved the fear temporarily and repressed the fearful dream. Thus we are left with an unresolved conflict as well as negative and unhealthy feelings. On the other hand, staying with the nightmare and accepting the challenge, as lucidity makes possible, allows us to resolve the dream problem in a fashion that leaves us more healthy than before. (184)

A person who, for example, is plagued by nightmares of being chased by a huge monster could thus use lucid dreaming to stop running away from the monster, turn around, and confront it. In this way the person could get a better understanding of what the monster *is* (i.e., what "monstrous" part of internal or external reality it symbolizes) and how to deal with it more positively.

LaBerge also suggests that lucid dreaming can offer people a means of spiritual growth and discovery. He describes traditional yogic practices of Tibetan Buddhists that concentrate on developing a "comprehension" of the illusory nature of the dream state; this comprehension is then generalized to the waking state, revealing the truth that all of reality is ultimately illusory. For modern Westerners, LaBerge says that lucid dreaming can lead to the same basic spiritual insights as those of Tibetan Buddhism:

Lucid dreaming can be a point of departure from which to understand how we might not be fully awake—for as ordinary dreaming is to lucid dreaming, so the ordinary waking state might be to the fully awakened state. This capacity of lucid dreams, to prepare us for a fuller awakening, may prove to be lucid dreaming's most significant potential for helping us become more alive in our lives. (279)

THE SENOI CONTROVERSY: KILTON STEWART AND G. WILLIAM DOMHOFF

A key reference source in the books of Faraday, Garfield, Taylor, and (to a lesser extent[1]) Delaney is an article by Kilton Stewart titled "Dream Theory in Malaya." The article was originally published in 1953, but it reached a vastly wider audience when it was reprinted in Charles Tart's best-selling anthology *Altered States of Consciousness* (1969). In this article Stewart describes his encounter with the dream beliefs and practices of the Senoi, a small tribal culture in Malaysia that he first learned of in 1935 while traveling with a scientific expedition. Stewart reports that the Senoi people enjoyed a remarkably pleasant and conflict-free life, with no violence, crime, or warfare to speak of. He attributes this astonishing degree of social and psychological harmony among the Senoi to their practice of sophisticated dream education and interpretation techniques. According to Stewart,

Dream interpretation is a feature of child education and is the common knowledge of all Senoi adults. The average Senoi layman practices the psychotherapy of dream interpretation on his family and his associates as a regular feature of education and daily social intercourse. Breakfast in the Senoi house is like a dream clinic, with the father and older brothers listening to and analyzing the dreams of all the children. At the end of the family clinic the male population gathers in the council, at which the dreams of the older children and all the men in the community are reported, discussed, and analyzed. (193)

The Senoi teach their children that within their dreams they should always "advance and attack in the teeth of danger," fighting against antagonistic dream characters and calling for help from dream allies when necessary (195). Children are also taught to force their dream antagonists to give them a gift (e.g., a story, a song, a dance) that the children can then share with the whole community upon awakening. In these ways, Senoi children are taught to value their inner creativity, to develop a strong sense of self-confidence, and to become an active contributor to the well-being of the group.

Stewart illustrates these teachings with the story of a Senoi boy who dreamed that he was attacked by a friend. Upon awakening the boy's father told him to describe the dream to his friend, which he did. The friend's father then told his son that he may have inadvertently offended the dreamer without knowing it, and that he should give a present to the dreamer and try to be especially nice to him. The boy who had the dream was also instructed to fight back in future dreams, and to defeat any dream character that used his friend's image as a disguise.

Observing the idyllic life of these rain forest dwellers and their passionate devotion to their dreams, Stewart concludes that many of the ills of modern civilization are due to its failure to develop the kinds of creative dream awareness that are central to the Senoi culture. But Stewart also concludes that the Senoi techniques are ultimately so simple that anyone can grasp them. He writes that, "fifteen years of experimentation with these Senoi principles have convinced me that all men, regardless of their cultural development, might profit by studying them" (193). Stewart devoted much of the rest of his life to translating what he had learned from the Senoi into terms that he felt ordinary Westerners could understand.

Stewart's account of Senoi dream theory had a huge impact on the emerging popular psychology approach to dreaming. The appealing image of a "primitive" people who lived in a virtual paradise because of their careful attention to dreams gave powerful inspiration to many people in Western society who were just beginning to explore their own dream experiences. Garfield, who visited the Senoi in 1972, captures this mood of excitement in her *Creative Dreaming*: "By applying Senoi concepts of dream control, we can produce beautiful creations and solve problems at the same time as integrating our personalities. . . . Perhaps the Senoi peacefulness, cooperation, and creativity will become more of a reality too!" (111)

However, some scholars questioned the quality of Stewart's research, and in 1985 G. William Domhoff published *The Mystique of Dreams*, a critical analysis of Stewart's claims in the light of other anthropological research on the Senoi. Domhoff argues that Stewart romanticized the Senoi and attributed to them beliefs and practices they never actually held. Like many cultures around the world, the Senoi pay attention to their dreams; but Domhoff asserts that there is no evidence the Senoi held "morning dream clinics" or taught principles of dream control to their children, as Stewart had claimed. Domhoff says,

There seems to be no way, then, to avoid a rather mundane conclusion after weighing a great deal of anthropological evidence from a variety of sources: Senoi people do not have an unusual theory or practice of dreams. . . . The Senoi do not practice the so-called Senoi dream theory. (34, 65)

Domhoff explains the appeal of "Senoi dream theory" first of all as a product of Stewart's own charismatic personality and story-telling abilities. He grants that Stewart "may have come to the ideas [about dream control, etc.] in part from discussions with dream adepts in Senoi settlements, but the ideas were in fact his" (64). Despite his failings as an anthropologist, Stewart earns Domhoff's respect as a man who was passionately committed to using his knowledge of the ritual practices of primitive peoples to help answer the terrible problems of modern society. "For all his foibles," Domhoff says, "there is a magic about Kilton Stewart that transcends Senoi dream theory" (64).

Domhoff also offers a broader explanation for all the excitement over the Senoi, an explanation which refers to the nature of American society in the 1960s and 1970s. Domhoff traces the widespread acceptance of Stewart's writings about the Senoi to three sources: the human potential movement (centered at the Esalen Institute in Big Sur, California), which publicized Senoi practices as a means to expanded consciousness and greater social harmony; protests against the Vietnam war, which focused attention on the acute differences between American culture and the cultures of southeast Asia; and the glowing endorsements of popular psychologists like Ann Faraday and Patricia Garfield. Domhoff says that ultimately the Senoi became a kind of allegory for many people living in this turbulent period of history:

Paradoxical as it may sound, I think that Senoi dream theory had a deep appeal for Americans at this time because it was a new application of our deepest and most ingrained beliefs about human nature presented in the context of an allegorical story about community and authenticity. Very simply, the "Senoi way of dreaming" actually rests on the unquestioned American belief in the possibility of shaping and controlling both the environment and human nature. For Americans, but not for most people, and certainly not for the Senoi, human nature is malleable and perfectible. We are what we make of ourselves. We can do it if we try. Senoi dream theory is an extension of that basic precept to the world of dreams. The fact that it is unwittingly presented in a mystique of the primitive only makes it all the more attractive. It is independent evidence for our convictions. (75)

The debate about Stewart, the Senoi, and "Senoi dream theory" continues to the present. Jeremy Taylor, for instance, argues that the anthropological reports cited by Domhoff were gathered after World War II, that is, after the Senoi culture had been ravaged by the violent intervention of foreign armies. Thus, Taylor doubts that the Senoi gave honest accounts to these later anthropologists about their real dream practices and beliefs. He asks,

if a group of superiorly armed foreigners from a totally different culture descended on your community and stuck you and your family in a stockade for a couple of years and actively prevented you from living your life the way you had always chosen to, would you be likely to "tell all" to those foreigners about your most intimate psycho-spiritual life and practices afterwards? I know I wouldn't, and I am not willing to assume any less about "native informants." (Taylor 1995, 32)

In the introduction to the second edition of her book *Pathway to Ecstasy* (1989), Garfield responds to Domhoff's criticism by saying that the truth about the Senoi will probably never be known; for her, the important thing is that "the principles attributed to the Senoi are effective" (xxv). She, Taylor, and many other popular psychologists agree that that whatever the Senoi originally practiced, the principles of dream control described by Kilton Stewart can be fruitfully applied by ordinary people living in modern Western society.

POPULAR PSYCHOLOGY'S ANSWERS TO THE THREE BASIC QUESTIONS

Formation

Popular psychologists believe that all humans have dreams: dreaming is a normal, natural part of every person's life. This belief is based on the traditional teachings of cultures from around the world, on the findings of the modern sleep laboratory, and on the experiences of popular psychologists in working closely with countless members of the general public. Popular psychologists generally agree that dreams are formed out of material from people's ordinary, daily life activities. They also agree that consciousness can play a large role in influencing and controlling dream content (e.g., in the cases of lucid dreaming and dream incubation). However, popular psychologists do not all agree on where the ultimate source of dream formation lies. Some, like Delaney and LaBerge, believe that dreams are created by the dreamer's mind alone; others, like Faraday, Garfield, and Taylor, believe that at least some dreams are shaped by transpersonal forces.

Function

For popular psychologists, dreams have the potential to serve a variety of positive functions in the lives of ordinary people. Although each of the popular psychologists discussed in this chapter emphasizes some dream functions more than others, they all claim that dreams work to give deep insights into a person's emotional world, help solve important problems in daily life, provide indications about physical health (even offering early warnings about impending illnesses), promote the overall integration of one's personality, stimulate creativity, imagination, and powers of original thought, and reveal profound spiritual truths. Most popular psychologists also discuss the possibility that a greater awareness of dreams can promote not just individual welfare but also the resolution of problems and conflicts that afflict society as a whole.

Interpretation

Popular psychologists focus most of their attention on giving detailed, practical instructions on how to interpret dreams. These instructions usually include advice on keeping a dream diary, suggestions about what typical dream themes frequently mean, and various techniques for connecting or bridging dream images to waking-life concerns. Most popular psychologists also describe how to practice dream incubation, how to become lucid while dreaming, how to share and interpret dreams in a group setting, and how to express and honor dream images in waking life. The popular psychology approach to dream interpretation is guided by the twin spirits of eclecticism and democracy: eclecticism in its willingness to use multiple methods of interpretation and its refusal to accept any one method as the best for all dreams and all dreamers; and democracy in its belief that everyone has the ability to interpret and benefit from his or her own dreams, without the need for analysts, therapists, scientists, priests, or any other supposed experts.

NOTE

1. In *Living Your Dreams* Delaney includes a discussion of Stewart's article on the Senoi (pp. 160-161), but makes a point of speaking of the "Stewart technique" rather than of the "Senoi technique"; in a footnote she expresses skepticism about the validity of Stewart's findings.

Chapter 8

Modern Psychology's Answers to the Three Basic Questions about Dreaming

I'm in Bosnia, in a house, on the second floor. A soldier below is firing a machine gun up through the floor, and I see bullets ripping up through the carpet all around me. I think I'm supposed to be some kind of peacekeeper; but I'm not very effective, I feel. I suddenly see lots of kids in the hallway, and I realize they're in real danger. So I slowly move them to a room that seems safe—but it's not. "Let's go upstairs," I say, and try to lead them up. But they don't follow me, and I end up only bringing their toys as I go up myself. Up above there is a big, grand living room, with beautiful old tapestries on the wall. A group of adults are sitting in plush chairs. They're in denial about the war, I think to myself. I say or do something that reminds them, though, and they get mad. Through a window I see the facades of a nearby building starting to crumble and fall down.

Kelly Bulkeley, June 24, 1995

One good way of evaluating the many different psychological theories about dreams and dreaming is to apply each of them in turn to a dream of one's own. Such an exercise brings forth the distinctive features of each theory and allows for critical reflection on their relative strengths and weaknesses. As this book has shown, the modern psychology of dreaming has grown in large part out of people's careful, disciplined examination of their own dreams. Beginning with the pioneering self-analyses of Freud and Jung, psychologists have regularly drawn on their own dreams as one important resource in pursuing their research. This does, it must be admitted, give dream psychology the appearance of being subjective and unscientific. But the unavoidable empirical fact is that our most direct means of access to the images, sensations, and emotions found in dreams is through our own dreams. Although debate about proper research methodology continues, most dream psychologists agree that if self-analysis is combined with solid findings from other research methods, there is nothing dangerous or unscientific about examining one's own dreams. Indeed, the history of modern dream psychology has demonstrated that many of the most creative new breakthroughs have come from researchers who have taken innovative approaches to their personal dream experiences.

PSYCHOLOGICAL ANALYSES OF A SAMPLE DREAM

Background

I had the above dream in June of 1995 while staying at a hotel in New York City. Although I enjoy the cultural vitality of New York, I have always disliked its noisy, manic urban atmosphere. I was there for the annual conference of the Association for the Study of Dreams, a group in which I was playing several administrative roles, and I was very busy with the conference all week long. Two or three times during the week, while making brief visits back to my hotel room, I saw a television news report on an especially vicious bombing in the war-torn land of Bosnia. The report showed a man carrying away the bloodied body of a little girl who had been killed in the bombing. In part because I have a two-year old daughter of my own, the horrible television image made me want to cry each time I saw it.

The dream came the last day of the conference, on Saturday night (actually, right before I woke up Sunday morning). Saturday afternoon I had presided over a long, contentious meeting of the association's board of directors. One particular issue had caused deep conflict within the group, and I felt I hadn't done a very good job of resolving it. Immediately after the board meeting a psychotherapist colleague and I went out to dinner with two literary agents to discuss our proposal for a parenting-genre book on children's dreams. The agents were very encouraging and agreed with us that a book describing how dreams can help nurture the growth and creativity of children would appeal to the parenting book market. Although I was excited by the project, I secretly worried that writing a commercial book might create conflicts with the scholarly standards and ideals that had guided my other writings.

The next day I was leaving New York to meet my wife and two children in Chicago. We were going to visit and stay with relatives who live in a large, well-furnished, multistoried house. Before going to sleep I told the friend with whom I was sharing my hotel room how nervous and apprehensive I always feel before such family gatherings.

Freud

A Freudian approach to the dream would begin with these memories and associations and would use them as clues to finding the repressed unconscious wishes motivating the dream. Although an exhaustive analysis of these associations is impractical here (Freud's line-by-line examination of his "Dream of Irma's Injection" runs fourteen pages), the following dream elements seem most striking. The image of the machine gun firing upward can be seen as a classic phallic symbol, an emblem of violent masculine desire and rage. The image of the children is a condensation of many different elements: my own children, the dead child from Bosnia, the children I will be discussing in my parenting book, my own experiences in childhood, and the child-like impulses still within me now. All of my action in the manifest dream is motivated by a deep fear that the Bosnian children are in danger. A Freudian reading might see my busy dream actions as a deceptive mask struggling to hide its unconscious opposite, a fear that *adults* are in danger—the ultimate unconscious wish behind the dream might in fact be an oedipal desire to kill my father. Such a terrible wish is too shocking to be accepted by my conscious ego, which is committed to the moral ideal of honoring and respecting my parents. So the censor has transformed that dark, repressed wish into the (superficially) less disturbing manifest imagery: casting the drama in a faraway land, where the adults are all just fine and where the children are the ones in danger. But the end of the dream indicates that the struggle between the unconscious wishes and conscious ideals is threatening to break out into the open, as the nearby building's facade (the exact image Freud used to describe how the manifest dream hides the latent wishes) is starting to crumble and fall down.

Jung

From a Jungian perspective, the first step would be to amplify the dream's elements and images, seeking evidence of unconscious compensations for the imbalances of my conscious attitudes. The architectural imagery in the dream could, somewhat like Jung's house dream (described in Chapter 3), be seen as a symbolic map of my intrapsychic condition. The soldier on the ground floor is a shadow figure, a deeply unconscious, unintegrated part of my psyche which my conscious ego sees as violent, destructive, and dangerous. The adults on the top floor are persona figures, comfortable in their elevated position of wealth and social status, refusing to pay any attention to the brutal warfare below. And the children trapped on the middle floor symbolize the youthful potentials and creative energies within me, the future growth of which is threatened by this terrible split between the "upper" and "lower" parts of my psyche. This dream would, in a Jungian view, be revealing to me that the exciting experiences in New York City, at the conference, and with the literary agents had combined to create an unhealthy imbalance in my psyche. Such an imbalance is endangering my ability to care for children both "inside" me (my inner potentials) and "outside" me (my own two children, the children who will be the subject of my book, the children of Bosnia). The dream tries to compensate for this excessive waking-life concern with my persona by bringing up archetypal symbols and vivid emotions from the unconscious.

Adler

An Adlerian approach would take this dream as a reflection of efforts to defend my sense of superiority and self-worth. Looking at the associations to the dream, it appears that the very difficult board meeting held the afternoon preceding the dream had deeply shaken my sense of superiority. I had tried, and failed, to resolve a bitter conflict among the board members, and I was feeling depressed and helpless about the situation. The dream, in this view, would have been formed in response to that waking-life difficulty, which my customary style of life had been unable to manage. The dream transformed my real problem (the board meeting conflict) into a fantasy problem (the Bosnian war) and thereby allowed me to use one of my customary strategies for defending against threats to my sense of superiority—the strategy of detaching myself, "rising above it all," as I do in the dream when I leave the children behind and go upstairs to the grand living room. I could not use this strategy with my waking life problem, but my dream alters the problem so that now the strategy *will* work. In Adlerian terms, the dream serves its function of preserving my sense of superiority and self-esteem, albeit without giving me any real help with the waking life problem.

Boss

From Boss's existentialist perspective dreams disclose aspects of our being-in-the-world, showing both unhealthy constrictions in our present life and wonderful potentials for our future. In this dream, the sensation of being trapped is very powerful. By focusing on the dream phenomenon itself, as Boss counsels, I see that the emotions of fear, vulnerability, and helplessness predominate. The dream indicates that this trapped mode of being-in-the-world is evident in many areas of my life (being in New York City, dealing with the board meeting conflict, writing the commercial book, going to visit my Chicago family). Boss would say that the dream is a real, genuine experience of being trapped—not a mere symbol or image, but an actual experience of that mode of being-in-the-world. However, the dream also reveals some real potentials for free choice and action. When I go upstairs and find the adults sitting in their plush chairs, I "say or do something" that reminds them of the war below; at that moment the facades start falling. This suggests that through consciousness and honest self-reflection I can break through the denial of my trapped condition, and thereby open up new potentials for the future.

French and Fromm

The Ego Psychological approach of French and Fromm looks at every dream as an attempt by the ego to solve a pressing concern in waking life, what they term the focal conflict. In this dream the focal conflict could be seen as the worries I have over writing the book on children's dreams. I'm afraid of the harm my ideals could suffer from the violent, war-like competition of commercial publishing (the soldier below), and yet I'm also afraid of the insulated, self-satisfied nature of academic writing (the adults above). My ego is caught in the middle, trying yet failing to be a peacekeeper and protect the core concern of the book, that is, the concern to help children learn from their dreams. The dream draws on many different elements from my life (the television news report, the upcoming family visit, the board meeting) in an attempt to master this focal conflict. French and Fromm would sift through my activities in the dream and distinguish the ineffective efforts to master the focal conflict (e.g., trying to hide the children somewhere on the second floor) from more effective efforts (e.g., making the adults on the third floor acknowledge the war below).

Perls

For Perls, dreams reveal holes in the Gestalt of our personalities and confront us with alienated, disowned parts of ourselves. In this dream, the soldier downstairs firing the machine gun upward appears to be the most alienated of all the characters. By experientially identifying with him, as Perls recommends, I hear the soldier say this: "I'm angry, I've been neglected and forgotten and now I'm going to make sure people pay attention to me. I know people are up there above me, and while they pretend I'm not here I'll shoot my gun until they hear me." The adults in the living room say this: "We're older, we need to rest. We've worked hard all our lives, and we've earned the right to enjoy some peace and comfort. We've built and preserved this society, and we won't tolerate rowdies who simply want to tear it all down." This is a classic example of what Perls calls a topdog versus underdog conflict. To follow his method, I would continue this dialogue between the soldier and the adults, bring in the other elements from the dream (e.g., the children, the house, the toys, the building facades), and work to understand them all as parts of myself, parts that need to be recognized, appreciated, and integrated.

Aserinsky, Kleitman, Dement

Although I did not have this dream while attached to an EEG monitor in a sleep laboratory, it was almost certainly a dream experienced during REM sleep. The dream is fairly long, with lots of visual imagery, physical activity, and emotional involvement. As I woke up early Sunday morning with this dream fresh and vivid in my mind, it seems likely that it came during the long REM period that for most humans occurs at the end of each night's sleep cycle.

Hobson

For Hobson, dreaming is activated by the random, chaotic neural activities of REM sleep. Higher mental functions then struggle to synthesize these bizarre inputs into a partly-coherent sequence of images and events. My dream certainly begins with an image of chaos and confusion, in the form of the soldier firing a machine gun upward (in his book *The Dreaming Brain* Hobson uses this very metaphor of random gunfire to describe the REM sleep neural activation that initiates the formation of a dream). The dream can then be seen as struggling to make some kind of sense out of these initially chaotic perceptions and feelings. I envision myself as being in a war, as needing to protect children; I try different strategies to get out of danger and restore peace. The dream becomes progressively calmer and more orderly as I go upstairs into the world of rational adult society, indicating that my higher mental functions are slowly gaining control over the mental chaos or "warfare" generated by REM sleep. For Hobson there is no coded message here, no deep unconscious wisdom. The dream has simply responded to the random neural inputs of REM sleep by creating a semi-logical narrative that revolves around my ordinary waking concerns with caring for children.

Crick and Mitchison

The reverse-learning theory of Crick and Mitchison holds that REM sleep works to remove negative, parasitic modes of behavior from the brain. Following their view I should just forget my dream, because trying to remember and interpret it might preserve unhealthy patterns of thought that it is the function of REM sleep to eliminate.

Hall

Hall's quantitative approach would begin by analyzing this dream into its basic structural elements (setting, characters, interactions, objects, and emotions). Briefly, a content analysis of this dream would categorize the setting as indoors, of questionable familiarity (I'm familiar with Bosnia, but not with this particular house). The characters, all unknown to me, include one adult male, a group of children of both sexes, and a group of adults of both sexes. The interactions include two aggressive ones (the soldier firing the machine gun, the adults getting mad at me) and two friendly ones (me trying to move the children out of danger, me trying to remind the adults of what's going on below). The objects include the house, the machine gun, the bullets, the carpet, the toys, the tapestries, and the building facade. And the two instances of emotion in the dream are the apprehension I feel about the children being in danger and the anger the adults feel toward me. After scoring the dream in this way, it could then be compared both to a longer series of my dreams and to data on the dreams of other people. This would enable me to determine how often in my dreams I feel apprehension, how frequently I succeed or fail in protecting children, how many known versus unknown characters appear in my dreams, and so forth. From Hall's perspective, the events, emotions, and activities in this dream are likely to be continuous with basic features of my waking life. For example, the multistoried house may be directly connected to the home of my Chicago relatives; the war in Bosnia could thus be seen as a simple mental shorthand for the emotional conflict I feel when I visit there.

Foulkes

For Foulkes, dreams carry no specific message or intent to communicate. However, he says dreams are shaped by the same logical processes of order, coherence, and association that govern all thought. In my dream, evidence of such processes can be seen in my realistic response to the danger posed by the soldier, in my verbal interactions with the children, and in the plausible, well-structured quality of the scene in the upstairs living room. These instances of rational thought demonstrate that no matter how bizarre dreams initially appear, on closer analysis it can be shown that they are shaped by the ordinary cognitive processes that experimental psychologists have found operating in both waking and sleeping mentation.

Hunt

There is a multiplicity of dream types, according to Hunt, and each different type is formed by a different combination of cognitive processes. Although my dream does not fit easily into any of Hunt's categories (it comes closest to his definition of a nightmare), it does reflect the influence of both sophisticated grammatical structures and creative visual-spatial imagery. The grammatical structures can be seen in the overall narrative coherence of the dream, with the action moving progressively from the lower to the upper stories of the house. The creative visual-spatial imagery emerges with the suddenly appearing sight of the nearby building's facade crumbling to pieces. Hunt would likely view this last image not as another bit of REM-generated nonsense with no meaningful connection to the preceding dream action, but as a visual-spatial image that enriches and completes the developing narrative thrust of the dream: as I reach the top floor of this house and find it to be filled with an air of luxurious, self-satisfied denial, I look outside and see the facade of another building falling down.

Hartmann

I have had frequent nightmares for most of my life, usually one or two a month but sometimes as often as two or three a week. Hartmann's theory that people with frequent nightmares have thin psychological boundaries applies to my personality in a number of ways (e.g., in terms of my interpersonal relations, my gender identity, my interest in fantasy). Looking at the nightmarish qualities of this particular dream, it appears that many of the actions and emotions revolve around threats to boundaries. The bullets ripping up through the floor violently attack a boundary, the denial of the adults anxiously tries to preserve a boundary, and the crumbling facade on the nearby building show the collapse of a boundary.

Faraday, Garfield, Delaney, Ullman, Taylor, LaBerge

Popular psychologists offer a variety of practical techniques for exploring a dream's meanings. To start with, they recommend carefully studying each image in the dream. For example, using Delaney's "pretend I'm from another planet" method, I would describe toys as objects which can be played with, which are fun and make you laugh; children can make a toy out of pretty much anything. That description makes me reflect anew on the opulent yet lifeless scene upstairs in the living room. Without children to play with them, toys are mere objects; without vitality and openness (which children have in abundance), all the lovely tapestries and plush furnishings of this living room are but decorations for a tomb. Popular psychologists would also recommend trying to incubate a future dream to gain further insights into this one (e.g., by going to sleep with the question, "How can I make true peace between the soldier on the ground floor and the adults on the upper floor?"); and in future dreams they would suggest I try to become lucid, so I could confront antagonists like the soldier and find out who he is and what he wants. Finally, popular psychologists would encourage me to share this dream with other people and seek their comments and reflections. Using Taylor's "if it were my dream" method, I would ask different people what such a dream would mean to them if they had experienced it.

Such an exercise in comparative dream analysis cannot, of course, do full justice to any of the individual theories. A thorough Jungian dream interpretation, for example, would require a far more detailed probing of the dreamer's personal life and a much broader amplification of the dream's archetypal symbolism than I have provided. Likewise, an adequate Hall and Van de Castle-style content analysis would demand the careful scoring of a long series of my dreams. But the primary goal of the above exercise has been more modest than that, namely to give readers a clear and concrete illustration of how the different psychological theories presented in this book would go about explaining and interpreting a sample dream.

MAJOR AREAS OF DEBATE

A second goal of this comparative dream analysis is to highlight the major areas of debate among psychological theories of dreaming. Despite (or perhaps because of) almost one hundred years of concentrated study, modern psychologists disagree on many fundamental points about the formation, function, and interpretation of dreams.

Formation

There are at least three major debates regarding the formation of dreams. First, what is the nature of the unconscious forces that work to form our dreams? Are these forces dark and destructive (Freud), or are they positive, creative, and even spiritual in nature (Jung)? Second, can dream formation be explained without using the imprecise notion of "the unconscious"? Many psychologists (Adler, Boss, Piaget, Hall) argue that a better explanation of dream formation refers to those same basic structures of personality and cognition that operate in our waking lives. Third, what is the role of REM sleep physiology in the formation of dreams? Some psychologists (Hobson, Crick and Mitchison) assert that the neural activities of REM sleep dominate the process of dream formation, while other psychologists (Foulkes, Hartmann, Hunt, LaBerge) see a complex interaction of REM physiology and cognitive-emotional forces at work in the formation of dreams.

Function

There are three basic positions on the question of what function dreams serve. The first position (Freud, Adler) is that dreams function to deceive consciousness, masking unpleasant truths and thereby preserving our customary psychological defenses. The second position (Jung, Boss, French and Fromm, Perls, Hartmann, Hunt, all popular psychologists) is that dreams serve a variety of highly positive functions: giving deep insights into neglected thoughts and emotions, helping solve important problems in daily life, stimulating creativity and imagination, and promoting the overall integration of personality. The third position (Hobson, Crick and Mitchison, Foulkes) is that dreams have little or no psychological function beyond a modest value in diagnosing psychological disturbances. In this latter view the real functions are served not by dreaming but by REM sleep, in its role of providing routine maintenance of basic neurological circuitry in the brain.

Interpretation

Those who see no psychological function to dreams naturally have little interest in trying to interpret dreams. Those who do believe that dreams serve some psychological function approach the process of interpretation from a number of different directions. (1) Most psychologists (following Freud) insist that any dream interpretation must begin with the personal associations of the dreamer. Some (Jung) also seek amplifications to the dream's images and symbols. However, others (Boss) reject associations and amplifications and say that interpretation should focus exclusively on the dreamer's experience itself. Still others (Hall) argue that even the dreamer is unnecessary, because nothing more than a series of written dream reports is required to make valid interpretations. (2) Many psychologists (Freud, Jung, Adler, Boss, French and Fromm) regard the aid of a trained psychotherapist as a valuable or even essential part of dream interpretation. Other psychologists (Hall, Faraday, Garfield, Delaney) disagree, saying that with a little practice any person can learn to interpret his or her own dreams. And for some (Perls, Ullman, Taylor), the ideal setting for dream interpretation is neither one-to-one psychotherapy nor private reflection and journal writing, but a dream sharing group. (3) Some psychologists (Freud, Hall) argue that dream interpretation can be precise, objective, and scientific in its results. Most other psychologists, however, believe that dream interpretation is more of an intuitive art in which many complex, multivalent meanings emerge out of each dream.

MODERN PSYCHOLOGY'S ANSWERS IN THE CONTEXT OF WESTERN HISTORY

As a final way of evaluating the answers given by modern psychologists to the three basic questions, they may be compared to the answers given earlier in Western history to the same questions.

The Bible

A number of modern psychologists (Jung, Boss, Hunt, Faraday, Garfield, Taylor) basically agree with the Bible that at least some of our dreams are formed by God, or by other divine, supernatural, or transpersonal forces. The theories of these psychologists also correspond closely to the Bible's portrayal of dream functions as providing spiritual revelations, prophecies of the future, and warnings of possible danger relevant to individuals and the broader community. And almost all psychologists agree with the Bible that while the best dream interpretations are guided by a kind of intuitive inspiration, it is very easy to misinterpret dreams if we are not careful in our analyses and reflections.

Aristotle

A large number of modern psychologists, perhaps the majority, follow Aristotle (and the more skeptical voices found in the Bible) in arguing that dreams are formed by the dreamer's own sleeping mind. Aristotle's rationalistic view that dreams have no specific function is clearly mirrored in the theories of many modern psychologists (Hobson, Crick and Mitchison, Foulkes). But like many of those psychologists, Aristotle believes that dreams, while not intentional messages from the gods, may still be read for useful information about the dreamer's life. His dictum that becoming a skillful interpreter of dreams requires learning how to observe resemblances could be taken as the cardinal law of all modern psychological dream interpretation, from Freud onward.

Artemidorus

Echoes of Artemidorus, particularly his thoughts about the function and interpretation of dreams, can be heard in the theories of many modern psychologists (Freud, Jung, Hall). But the approach of Artemidorus is most closely related to the work of popular psychologists: the disinclination to engage in theological debates about where dreams come from, the deep interest in dreams as bearing messages that can be used to improve the waking lives of ordinary people, and the interpretive methods of carefully examining the dreamer's personal life, comparing specific dream images to common cultural symbols, and using one's own experience and native intelligence. In all these ways Artemidorus anticipates the basic attitudes, approaches, and techniques of popular psychologists.

It is beyond the scope of this book to examine in any further detail these historical influences and connections. My hope, however, is that readers will themselves go on to study the historical predecessors to the dream theories of modern psychologists (and, beyond that, to investigate the cross-cultural parallels to these theories). Because dreaming is both an intimate personal experience and a phenomenon found in all cultures and eras of history, it offers a wonderful pathway for people to explore and celebrate the shared yet infinitely varied humanity that unites every one of us.

Bibliography

Note: The best general resources for information on current research on the psychology of dreaming are (1) *Dreaming: The Journal of the Association for the Study of Dreams* (ASD, PO Box 1600, Vienna, VA 22183; ASDreams@aol.com); (2) *The Encyclopedia of Sleep and Dreaming*, ed. Mary Carskadon (New York: Macmillan, 1993); and (3) the volumes in the *Series in Dream Studies* edited by Robert Van de Castle, from State University of New York Press (SUNY Press, State University Plaza, Albany, NY 12246).

Adler, Alfred. 1956. *The Individual Psychology of Alfred Adler*. Edited by H. L. A. and R. R. Ansbacher. New York: Harper Torchbooks.

Alston, T., R. Calogeras, and H. Deserno, eds. 1993. *Dream Reader: Psychoanalytic Articles on Dreams*. New York: International Universities Press.

Aristotle. 1941a. On Dreams. In *The Collected Works of Aristotle*, edited by R. McKeon. New York: Random House.

——— 1941b. On Prophesying by Dreams. In *The Collected Works of Aristotle*, edited by R. McKeon. New York: Random House.

Armitage, R. 1992. Gender Differences and the Effect of Stress on Dream Recall: A 30-Day Diary Report. *Dreaming* 2(3): 137-142.

Artemidorus. 1975. *Oneirocriticon*. Translated by R. J. White. Park Ridge, NJ: Noyes Press.

Aserinsky, E., and N. Kleitman. 1953. Regularly Occurring Periods of Eye Motility, and Concomitant Phenomena, during Sleep. *Science* 118: 273-274.

Aserinsky, E., and N. Kleitman. 1955. Two Types of Ocular Motility Occurring in Sleep. *Journal of Applied Physiology* 8: 1-10.

Baars, B., and W. Banks. 1994. Dream Consciousness: A Neurocognitive Approach. *Consciousness and Cognition* 3(1).

Bakan, D. 1958. *Sigmund Freud and the Jewish Mystical Tradition*. Boston: Beacon Press.

Barrett, D. 1991. Flying Dreams and Lucidity: An Empirical Study of Their Relationship. *Dreaming* 1(2): 129-134.

——— 1992. Just How Lucid are Lucid Dreams? *Dreaming* 2(4): 221-228.

——— 1994. Dreams in Dissociative Disorders. *Dreaming* 4(3): 165-176.

———— 1996. *Trauma and Dreams*. Cambridge, MA: Harvard University Press.

Bearden, C. 1994. The Nightmare: Biological and Psychological Origins. *Dreaming* 4(2): 139-152.

Beaudet, D. 1990. *Encountering the Monster: Pathways in Children's Dreams*. New York: Continuum.

Belicki, K. 1987. Recalling Dreams: An Examination of Daily Variation and Individual Differences. In *Sleep and Dreams: A Sourcebook*, edited by J. Gackenbach. New York: Garland.

Bell, A., and C. Hall. 1971. *The Personality of a Child Molester: An Analysis of Dreams*. Chicago: Aldine Atherton.

Beradt, C. 1966. *The Third Reich of Dreams*. Translated by A. Gottwald. Chicago: Quadrangle.

Berne, P., and L. Savary. 1991. *Dream Symbol Work*. Mahwah, NJ: Paulist Press.

Bernheimer, C., and C. Kahane, eds. 1985. *In Dora's Case: Freud-Hysteria-Feminism*. New York: Columbia University Press.

Binswanger, L. 1967. *Being in the World: Selected Papers of Ludwig Binswanger*. Translated by J. Needleman. New York: Harper Torchbooks.

———— 1993. Dream and Existence. In *Dream and Existence*, edited by K. Hoeller. Atlantic Highlands, NJ: Humanities Press.

Blagrove, M. 1992. Dreams as the Reflection of our Waking Concerns and Abilities: A Critique of the Problem-Solving Paradigm in Dream Research. *Dreaming* 2(4): 205-220.

Bonime, W., with F. Bonime. 1988. *The Clinical Use of Dreams*. New York: DeCapo Press.

Bosnak, R. 1988. *A Little Course in Dreams*. Boston: Shambhala.

———— 1989. *Dreaming with an AIDS Patient: An Intimate Look Inside the Dreams of a Gay Man with AIDS by His Analyst*. Boston: Shambhala.

———— 1996. *Tracks in the Wilderness of Dreaming: Exploring Interior Landscape Through Practical Dreamwork*. New York: Delacorte Press.

Boss, M. 1958. *The Analysis of Dreams*. New York: Philosophical Library.

———— 1977. *I Dreamt Last Night . . .* New York: Gardner.

Brenneis, C. 1975. Developmental Aspects of Aging in Women: A Comparative Study of Dreams. *Archives of General Psychiatry* 32: 429-434.

Brockway, S. S. 1987. Group Treatment of Combat Nightmares in Post-Traumatic Stress Disorder. *Journal of Contemporary Psychotherapy* 17: 270-284.

Brook, S., ed. 1987. *The Oxford Book of Dreams*. Oxford, England: Oxford University Press.

Bulkeley, K. 1991. Interdisciplinary Dreaming: Hobson's Successes and Failures. *Dreaming* 1(3): 225-234.

———— 1993. Dreaming is Play. *Psychoanalytic Psychology* 10(4): 501-514.

———— 1994. *The Wilderness of Dreams: Exploring the Religious Meanings of Dreams in Modern Western Culture*. Albany: State University of New York Press.

———— 1995. *Spiritual Dreaming: A Cross-Cultural and Historical Journey*. Mahwah, NJ: Paulist Press.

———— ed. 1996. *Among All These Dreamers: Essays on Dreaming and Modern Society*. Albany: State University of New York Press.

Bynum, E. B. 1993. *Families and the Interpretation of Dreams: Awakening the Intimate Web.* New York: Harrington Park Press.

Carskadon, M., ed. 1993. *Encyclopedia of Sleep and Dreaming.* New York: Macmillan.

Cartwright, R. 1979. *Night Life: Explorations in Dreaming.* Englewood Cliffs, NJ: Prentice-Hall.

———— 1991. Dreams that Work: The Relation of Dream Incorporation to Adaptation to Stressful Events. *Dreaming* 1(1): 3-10.

———— 1993. Who Needs Their Dreams? The Usefulness of Dreams in Psychotherapy. *Journal of the American Academy of Psychoanalysis* 21(4): 539-547.

Cartwright, R., and L. Lamberg. 1992. *Crisis Dreaming: Using Your Dreams to Solve Your Problems.* New York: HarperCollins.

Cartwright, R., S. Lloyd, S. Knight, and I. Trenholme. 1984. Broken Dreams: A Study of the Effects of Divorce and Depression on Dream Content. *Psychiatry* 47: 251-259.

Catalano, S. 1990. *Children's Dreams in Clinical Practice.* New York: Plenum Press.

Charsley, S. R. 1973. Dreams in an Independent African Church. *Africa: Journal of the International African Institute* 43(3): 244-257.

———— 1987. Dreams and Purposes: An Analysis of Dream Narratives in an Independent African Church. *Africa: Journal of the International African Institute* 57(3): 281-296.

Clark, R. W. 1980. *Freud: The Man and the Cause.* New York: Random House.

Clift, J. D., and W. B. Clift. 1986. *Symbols of Transformation in Dreams.* New York: Crossroad.

Clift, J. D., and W. B. Clift. 1991. *The Hero Journey in Dreams.* New York: Crossroad.

Covitz, J. 1990. *Visions of the Night: A Study of Jewish Dream Interpretation.* Boston: Shambhala.

Crapanzano, V. 1975. Saints, Jnun, and Dreams: An Essay in Moroccan Ethnopsychology. *Psychiatry* 38: 145-159.

Crick, F. and G. Mitchison. 1983. The Function of Dream Sleep. *Nature* 304: 111-114.

Cuddy, M. A., and K. Belicki. 1992. Nightmare Frequency and Related Sleep Disturbance as Indicators of a History of Sexual Abuse. *Dreaming* 2(1): 15-22.

Cuddy, M. A., and K. Belicki. 1996. The 55-Year Secret: Using Nightmares to Facilitate Psychotherapy in a Case of Childhood Sexual Abuse. In *Among All These Dreamers: Essays on Dreaming and Modern Society*, edited by K. Bulkeley. Albany: State University of New York Press.

Curley, R. T. 1983. Dreams of Power: Social Process in a West African Religious Movement. *Africa: Journal of the International African Institute* 53(3): 20-37.

Decker, H. 1991. *Freud, Dora, and Vienna 1900.* New York: Free Press.

Delaney, G. 1979. *Living Your Dreams.* New York: Harper and Row.

———— 1991. *Breakthrough Dreaming: How to Tap the Power of Your 24-Hour Mind.* New York: Bantam.

———— ed. 1993. *New Directions in Dream Interpretation.* Albany: State University of New York Press.

———— 1994. *Sexual Dreams: Why We Have Them and What They Mean.* New York: Fawcett Columbine.

Dement, W. 1960. The Effect of Dream Deprivation. *Science* 131: 1705-1707.

———— 1972. *Some Must Watch While Some Must Sleep: Exploring the World of Sleep.* New York: W. W. Norton.

Dement, W., and N. Kleitman. 1957a. The Relation of Eye Movements During Sleep to Dream Activity: An Objective Method for the Study of Dreaming. *Journal of Experimental Psychology* 53: 339-346.

Dement, W., and N. Kleitman. 1957b. Cyclic Variations in EEG During Sleep and their Relation to Eye Movements, Body Motility, and Dreaming. *Electroencephalography and Clinical Neurophysiology* 9: 673-690.

Dement, W., E. Kahn, and H. Roffwarg. 1965. The Influence of the Laboratory Situation on the Dreams of the Experimental Subject. *Journal of Nervous and Mental Disease* 149: 119-131.

Devereux, G., ed. 1953. *Psychoanalysis and the Occult.* New York: International Universities Press.

———— 1951. *Reality and Dream: Psychotherapy of a Plains Indian.* New York: International Universities Press.

———— 1975. *Dreams in Greek Tragedy: An Ethno-Psychoanalytic Study.* Berkeley: University of California Press.

Dombeck, M. T. 1991. *Dreams and Professional Personhood.* Albany: State University of New York Press.

Domhoff, G. W. 1985. *The Mystique of Dreams: A Search for Utopia Through Senoi Dream Theory.* Berkeley: University of California Press.

———— 1996. *Finding Meaning in Dreams: A Quantitative Approach.* New York: Plenum.

Doniger, W. 1996. Eastern Dreams About Western Dreams. In *Among All These Dreamers: Essays on Dreaming and Modern Society,* edited by K. Bulkeley. Albany: State University of New York Press.

Doniger, W., and K. Bulkeley. 1993. Why Study Dreams? A Religious Studies Perspective. *Dreaming* 3(1): 69-74.

Dudley, L., and J. Fungaroli. 1987. The Dreams of Students in a Women's College: Are They Different? *ASD Newsletter* 4(6): 6-7.

Dunlop, C., ed. 1977. *Philosophical Essays on Dreaming.* Ithaca, NY: Cornell University Press.

Eggan, D. 1952. The Manifest Content of Dreams: A Challenge to Social Science. *American Anthropologist* 54: 469-485.

———— 1955. The Personal Use of Myth in Dreams. *Journal of American Folklore* 68: 445-463.

Eggan, D. 1957. Hopi Dreams and a Life History Sketch. *Primary Records in Culture and Personality* 2(16): 1-147.

Ellenberger, H. 1970. *The Discovery of the Unconscious: The History and Evolution of Dynamic Psychiatry.* New York: Basic Books.

Ellman, S., ed. 1991. *The Mind in Sleep: Psychology and Psychophysiology.* Second ed. New York: Wiley.

Epel, N. 1993. *Writers Dreaming: Twenty-six Writers Talk About Their Dreams and the Creative Process.* New York: Crown.

Erikson, E. 1954. The Dream Specimen of Psychoanalysis. *Journal of the American Psychoanalytical Association* 2: 5-56.

Evans, C. 1983. *Landscapes of the Night: How and Why We Dream*. London, England: V. Gollancz.

Ewing, K. 1989. The Dream of Spiritual Initiation and the Organization of Self Representations among Pakistani Sufis. *American Ethnologist* 16: 56-74.

Fabian, J. 1966. Dreams and Charisma: "Theories of Dreams" in the Jamaa-Movement (Congo). *Anthropos* 61: 544-560.

Faraday, A. 1972. *Dream Power*. New York: Berkeley Books.

——— 1974. *The Dream Game*. New York: Harper and Row.

Firth, R. 1934. The Meaning of Dreams in Tikopia. In *Essays Presented to C. G. Seligman*, edited by E. E. Evans-Pritchard. London, England: Kegan Paul.

Flannery, R., and M. E. Chambers. 1985. Each Man Has His Own Friends: The Role of Dream Visitors in Traditional East Cree Belief and Practice. *Arctic Anthropology* 22(1): 1-22.

Fosshage, J.L. 1983. The Psychological Function of Dreams: A Revised Psychoanalytic Perspective. *Psychoanalysis and Contemporary Thought* 6(4): 641-670.

Fosshage, J. L., and C. A. Loew, eds. 1978. *Dream Interpretation: A Comparative Study*. New York: Spectrum.

Foucault, M. 1993. Dream, Imagination and Existence. In *Dream and Existence*, edited by K. Hoeller. Atlantic Highlands, NJ: Humanities Press.

Foulkes, D. 1962. Dream Reports from Different Stages of Sleep. *Journal of Abnormal and Social Psychology* 65: 14-25.

——— 1967. Dreams of a Male Child: Four Case Studies. *Journal of Child Psychology and Psychiatry* 8: 81-98.

——— 1971. Longitudinal Studies of Dreams in Children. In *Dream Dynamics: Scientific Proceedings of the American Academy of Psychoanalysis*, edited by J. H. Masserman. New York: Grune-Stratton.

——— 1978a. Dreams of Innocence. *Psychology Today* (December): 78-88.

——— 1978b. *A Grammar of Dreams*. New York: Basic Books.

——— 1979. Children's Dreams. In *Handbook of Dreams: Research, Theories, and Applications*, edited by B. B. Wolman. New York: Van Nostrand Reinhold.

——— 1982. *Children's Dreams: Longitudinal Studies*. New York: Wiley.

——— 1982b. A Cognitive-Psychological Model of REM Dream Production. *Sleep* 5(2): 169-187.

——— 1985. *Dreaming: A Cognitive-Psychological Analysis*. Hillsdale, NJ: L. Erlbaum.

French, T., and E. Fromm. 1964. *Dream Interpretation: A New Approach*. New York: Basic Books.

French, T., and E. Fromm. 1992. Formation and Evaluation of Hypotheses in Dream Interpretation. In *Essential Papers on Dreams*, edited by M. E. Lansky. New York: New York University Press.

Freud, S. 1953-1974. *Standard Edition of the Complete Psychological Works of Sigmund Freud*. Edited by J. Strachey. 24 vols. London: Hogarth Press.

——— 1953a. Dreams and Telepathy. In *Psychoanalysis and the Occult*, edited by G. Devereux. New York: International Universities Press.

——— 1953b. Psychoanalysis and Telepathy. In *Psychoanalysis and the Occult*, edited by G. Devereux. New York: International Universities Press.

——— 1953c. The Occult Significance of Dreams. In *Psychoanalysis and the Occult*, edited by G. Devereux. New York: International Universities Press.

——— 1963a. *Dora: Fragment of an Analysis of a Case of Hysteria*. Translated by P. Rieff. New York: Collier Books.

——— 1963b. Remarks upon the Theory and Practice of Dream Interpretation. In *Therapy and Technique*, edited by P. Rieff. New York: Collier Books.

——— 1963c. Some Additional Notes on Dream Interpretation as a Whole. In *Therapy and Technique*, edited by P. Rieff. New York: Collier Books.

——— 1965a. *The Interpretation of Dreams*. Translated by J. Strachey. New York: Avon.

——— 1965b. *New Introductory Lectures on Psychoanalysis*. Translated by J. Strachey. New York: W. W. Norton.

——— 1966. *Introductory Lectures on Psychoanalysis*. Translated by J. Strachey. New York: W. W. Norton.

——— 1980. *On Dreams*. Translated by J. Strachey. New York: W. W. Norton.

Frieden, K. 1990. *Freud's Dream of Interpretation*. Albany: State University of New York Press.

Fromm, E. 1951. *The Forgotten Language: An Introduction to the Understanding of Dreams, Fairy Tales, and Myths*. New York: Grove.

Gackenbach, J., ed. 1987. *Sleep and Dreams: A Source Book*. New York: Garland.

——— 1991. Frameworks for Understanding Lucid Dreaming: A Review. *Dreaming* 1(2): 109-128.

Gackenbach, J., and J. Bosveld. 1989. *Control Your Dreams*. New York: Harper and Row.

Gackenbach, J., and S. LaBerge, eds. 1988. *Conscious Mind, Sleeping Brain*. New York: Plenum.

Garber, M. B. 1974. *Dream in Shakespeare: From Metaphor to Metamorphosis*. New Haven, CT: Yale University Press.

Garfield, P. 1974. *Creative Dreaming*. New York: Ballantine.

——— 1985. *Your Child's Dreams*. New York: Ballantine.

——— 1988. *Women's Bodies, Women's Dreams*. New York: Ballantine.

——— 1989. *Pathway to Ecstasy: The Way of the Dream Mandala*. Second ed. Englewood Cliffs, NJ: Prentice Hall.

——— 1991. *The Healing Power of Dreams*. New York: Fireside Books.

Gay, P. 1988. *Freud: A Life for Our Time*. New York: W. W. Norton.

Gedo, J., and A. Goldberg. 1973. *Models of the Mind: A Psychoanalytic Theory*. Chicago: University of Chicago Press.

Gendlin, E. 1986. *Let Your Body Interpret Your Dreams*. Wilmette, IL: Chiron.

Gensler, D. 1994. Soliciting Dreams in Child Psychotherapy: The Influence of the Therapist's Interest. *Contemporary Psychoanalysis* 30(2): 367-383.

Gillespie, G. 1992. Light in Lucid Dreams: A Review. *Dreaming* 2(3): 167-180.

Globus, G. 1987. *Dream Life, Wake Life: The Human Condition Through Dreams*. Albany: State University of New York Press.

Gollnick, J. 1987. *Dreams in the Psychology of Religion*. New York: Edwin Mellen Press.

Green, C. 1968. *Lucid Dreams*. Oxford, England: Institute of Psychophysical Research.

Greenberg, R., R. Pillard, and C. Pearlman. 1972. The Effect of Dream (REM) Deprivation on Adaptation to Stress. *Psychosomatic Medicine* 34: 257-262.

Gregor, T. 1981a. "Far, Far Away My Shadow Wandered . . .": The Dream Symbolism and Dream Theories of the Mehinaku Indians of Brazil. *American Ethnologist* 8(4): 709-729.

———— 1981b. A Content Analysis of Mehinaku Dreams. *Ethos* 9: 353-390.

———— 1983. Dark Dreams about the White Man. *Natural History* 92(1): 8-14.

Grey, A., and D. Kalsched. 1971. Oedipus East and West: An Exploration Via Manifest Dream Content. *Journal of Cross-Cultural Psychology* 2: 337-352.

Grinstein, A. 1980. *Sigmund Freud's Dreams*. New York: International Universities Press.

Hall, C. 1966. *The Meaning of Dreams*. Revised ed. New York: McGraw-Hill.

———— 1967. Representation of the Laboratory Setting in Dreams. *Journal of Nervous and Mental Disease* 144: 198-206.

Hall, C., and G. W. Domhoff. 1963a. A Ubiquitous Sex Difference in Dreams. *Journal of Abnormal and Social Psychology* 66: 278-280.

———— 1963b. Aggression in Dreams. *International Journal of Social Psychiatry* 9: 259-267.

———— 1964. Friendliness in Dreams. *Journal of Social Psychology* 62: 309-314.

———— 1968. The Dreams of Freud and Jung. *Psychology Today*, June.

Hall, C., and R. Lind. 1970. *Dreams, Life, and Literature: A Study of Franz Kafka*. Chapel Hill: University of North Carolina Press.

Hall, C., and V. Nordby. 1972. *The Individual and His Dreams*. New York: Signet.

Hall, C., and R. Van de Castle. 1966. *The Content Analysis of Dreams*. New York: Appleton-Century-Crofts.

Hall, J. A. 1983. *Jungian Dream Interpretation*. New York: Inner City Books.

———— 1993. *The Unconscious Christian: Images of God in Dreams*. Mahwah, NJ: Paulist Press.

Hall, L. J. 1994. Experiential Dream Group Work from a Lay Perspective. *Dreaming* 4(4): 231-236.

Hallowell, A. I. 1966. The Role of Dreams in Ojibwa Culture. In *The Dream and Human Societies*, edited by G. E. Von Grunebaum and R. Callois. Berkeley: University of California Press.

Harris, M. 1994. *Studies in Jewish Dream Interpretation*. Northvale, NJ: Jason Aronson.

Hartmann, E. 1967. *The Biology of Dreaming*. Springfield, IL: Charles C. Thomas.

———— ed. 1970. *Sleep and Dreaming*. Boston: Little, Brown.

———— 1973. *The Functions of Sleep*. New Haven, CT: Yale University Press.

———— 1984. *The Nightmare: The Psychology and Biology of Terrifying Dreams*. New York: Basic Books.

———— 1991a. *Boundaries of the Mind: A New Psychology of Personality*. New York: Basic Books.

———— 1991b. Introductory Statement. *Dreaming* 1(1): 1-2.

———— 1995. Making Connections in a Safe Place: Is Dreaming Psychotherapy? *Dreaming* 5(4): 213-228.

Hartmann, E., R. Elkin, and M. Garg. 1991c. Personality and Dreaming: The Dreams of People with Very Thick or Very Thin Boundaries. *Dreaming* 1(4): 311-324.

Haskell, R. E. 1986. Cognitive Psychology and Dream Research: Historical, Conceptual, and Epistemological Considerations. *The Journal of Mind and Behavior* 7(2-3): 131-159.

Hill, M. O. 1994. *Dreaming the End of the World: Apocalypse as a Rite of Passage.* Dallas, TX: Spring.

Hillman, J. 1979. *The Dream and the Underworld.* New York: Harper and Row.

Hobson, J. A. 1988. *The Dreaming Brain: How the Brain Creates Both the Sense and the Nonsense of Dreams.* New York: Basic Books.

Hobson, J. A. and R. W. McCarley. 1977. The Brain as a Dream-State Generator: An Activation-Synthesis Hypothesis of the Dream Process. *American Journal of Psychiatry* 134: 1335-1368.

Hoeller, K., ed. 1993. *Dream and Existence.* Atlantic Highlands, NJ: Humanities Press.

Homans, P. 1979. *Jung in Context: Modernity and the Making of a Psychology.* Chicago: University of Chicago Press.

———— 1989. *The Ability to Mourn: Disillusionment and the Social Origins of Psychoanalysis.* Chicago: University of Chicago Press.

Hopcke, R. H. 1990. *Men's Dreams, Men's Healing: A Psychotherapist Explores a New View of Masculinity Through Jungian Dreamwork.* Boston: Shambhala.

Hunt, H. 1989. *The Multiplicity of Dreams: Memory, Imagination, and Consciousness.* New Haven, CT: Yale University Press.

Jedrej, M. C. and R. Shaw, eds. 1992. *Dreaming, Religion, and Society in Africa.* Leiden, The Netherlands: E. J. Brill.

Jones, E. 1951. *On the Nightmare.* New York: Liveright.

———— 1953-1957. *The Life and Work of Sigmund Freud.* 3 vols. New York: Basic Books.

Jones, R. 1978. *The New Psychology of Dreaming.* New York: Penguin.

———— 1962. *Ego Synthesis in Dreams.* Cambridge, MA: Schenkman.

Jung, C. G. 1965. *Memories, Dreams, Reflections.* Translated by R. Winston and C. Winston. New York: Vintage.

———— 1966. *The Practice of Psychotherapy.* Translated by R. Hull. Second ed. Princeton, NJ: Princeton University Press.

———— 1967. *The Collected Works of C. G. Jung.* Translated by R. Hull. Edited by W. McGuire. 20 vols. Princeton, NJ: Princeton University Press.

———— 1974. *Dreams.* Translated by R. Hull. Princeton, NJ: Princeton University Press.

———— 1984. *Dream Analysis: C. G. Jung Seminars, vol. 1.* Translated by R. Hull. Princeton, NJ: Princeton University Press.

Kagan, R. 1990. *Lucrecia's Dreams: The Politics of Prophesy in 16th Century Spain.* Berkeley: University of California Press.

Kane, C. R., P. Mellen, P. Patton, and I. Samano. 1993. Differences in the Manifest Dream Content of Mexican-American and Anglo-American Women: A Research Note. *Hispanic Journal of Behavioral Sciences* 5: 134-139.

Kellerman, H., ed. 1987. *The Nightmare: Psychological and Biological Foundations.* New York: Columbia University Press.

Kelsey, M. 1974. *God, Dreams, and Revelation: A Christian Interpretation of Dreams.* Minneapolis, MN: Augsburg.

———— 1978. *Dreams: A Way to Listen to God.* Mahwah, NJ: Paulist Press.

Kelzer, K. 1987. *The Sun and the Shadow.* New York: A. R. E. Press.

King, J., and K. Bulkeley. 1994. ASD Historical Committee Report. *ASD Newsletter* 11(4): 14-15, 22.

Koulack, D. 1991. *To Catch a Dream: Explorations of Dreaming.* Albany: State University of New York Press.

Kracke, W. 1979. Dreaming in Kagwahiv: Dream Beliefs and Their Psychic Uses in an Amazonian Indian Culture. *The Psychoanalytic Study of Society* 8: 119-171.

——— 1981. Kagwahiv Mourning: Dreams of a Bereaved Father. *Ethos* 9(4): 258-275.

——— 1987. Myths in Dreams, Thought in Images: An Amazonian Contribution to the Psychoanalytic Theory of Primary Process. In *Dreaming: Anthropological and Psychological Interpretations*, edited by B. Tedlock. New York: Cambridge University Press.

Krakow, B., and J. Neidhardt. 1992. *Conquering Bad Dreams and Nightmares.* New York: Berkeley Books.

Krakow, B., D. Tandberg, M. Barey, and L. Scriggins. 1995. Nightmares and Sleep Disturbance in Sexually Assaulted Women. *Dreaming* 5(3): 199-206.

Kramer, M. 1991. The Nightmare: A Failure in Dream Function. *Dreaming* 1(4): 277-286.

Krippner, S., ed. 1990. *Dreamtime and Dreamwork.* Los Angeles: Jeremy Tarcher.

Krippner, S., S. Gabel, S. Green, and R. Rubien. 1994. Community Applications of an Experiential Group Approach to Teaching Dreamwork. *Dreaming* 4(4): 215-222.

Krippner, S., and J. Dillard. 1988. *Dreamworking: How to Use Your Dreams for Creative Problem-Solving.* Buffalo, NY: Bearly.

Kuiken, D. 1995. Dreams and Feeling Realization. *Dreaming* 5(3): 129-158.

Kuiken, D., and L. Smith. 1991. Impactful Dreams and Metaphor Generation. *Dreaming* 1(2): 135-146.

LaBerge, S. 1985. *Lucid Dreaming.* Los Angeles: Jeremy Tarcher.

Lakoff, G. 1993. How Metaphor Structures Dreams: The Theory of Conceptual Metaphor Applied to Dream Analysis. *Dreaming* 3(2): 77-98.

Lansky, M., ed. 1992. *Essential Papers on Dreaming.* New York: New York University Press.

Lansky, M. R., and C. R. Bley. 1993. Exploration of Nightmares in Hospital Treatment of Borderline Patients. *Bulletin of the Menninger Clinic* 54: 466-477.

Lanternari, V. 1975. Dreams as Charismatic Significants: Their Bearing on the Rise of New Religious Movements. In *Psychological Anthropology*, edited by T. R. Williams. Paris: Mouton.

Laufer, B. 1931. Inspirational Dreams in Eastern Asia. *Journal of American Folk-Lore* 44: 208-216.

Lavie, P., and H. Kaminer. 1991. Dreams That Poison Sleep: Dreaming in Holocaust Survivors. *Dreaming* 1(1): 11-22.

Layard, J. 1988. *The Lady of the Hare: A Study in the Healing Power of Dreams.* Boston: Shambhala.

Levin, R., J. Galin, and B. Zywiak. 1991. Nightmares, Boundaries, and Creativity. *Dreaming* 1(1): 63-74.

Levine, J. 1991. The Role of Culture in the Representation of Conflict in Dreams: A Comparison of Bedouin, Irish, and Israeli Children. *Journal of Cross Cultural Psychology* 22(4): 472-490.

Lincoln, J. S. 1935. *The Dream in Primitive Cultures.* London: University of London.

Long, M.W. 1987. What is This Thing Called Sleep? *National Geographic* vol. 172, no. 6, 787-821.

Lortie-Lussier, M., S. Simond, N. Rinfret, and J. De Koninck. 1985. Working Mothers Versus Homemakers: Do Dreams Reflect the Changing Roles of Women? *Sex Roles* 12: 1009-1021.

Lortie-Lussier, M., S. Simond, N. Rinfret, and J. De Koninck. 1992. Beyond Sex Differences: Family and Occupational Roles' Impact on Women's and Men's Dreams. *Sex Roles* 26: 79-96.

Lowy, Samuel. 1942. *Psychological and Biological Foundations of Dream-Interpretation.* London: Kegan Paul, Trench, and Trubner.

Lynch, Kathryn L. 1988. *The High Medieval Dream Vision: Poetry, Philosophy, and Literary Form.* Stanford, CA: Stanford University Press.

Mack, J. E. 1970. *Nightmares and Human Conflict.* New York: Columbia University Press.

MacKenzie, N. 1965. *Dreams and Dreaming.* New York: Vanguard.

Malcolm, N. 1959. *Dreaming.* London: Routledge and Kegan Paul.

Masson, J. M., ed. 1985. *The Complete Letters of Sigmund Freud to Wilhelm Fliess, 1887-1904.* Cambridge, MA: Belknap.

Mattoon, M. A. 1978. *Understanding Dreams.* Dallas, TX: Spring.

Maybruck, P. 1989. *Pregnancy and Dreams.* Los Angeles: Jeremy Tarcher.

——— 1991. *Romantic Dreams: How to Enhance Your Romantic Relationship by Understanding and Sharing Your Dreams.* New York: Pocket Books.

McCaffrey, P. 1984. *Freud and Dora: The Artful Dream.* New Brunswick, NJ: Rutgers University Press.

McDonald, P. 1987. *Dreams: Night Language of the Soul.* New York: Continuum.

McGuire, W., ed. 1974. *The Freud/Jung Letters: The Correspondence Between Sigmund Freud and C. G. Jung.* Princeton, NJ: Princeton University Press.

Medici de Steiner, C. 1993. Children and Their Dreams. *International Journal of Psychoanalysis* 74(2): 359-370.

Meier, C. A. 1967. *Ancient Incubation and Modern Psychotherapy.* Translated by M. Curtis. Evanston, IL: Northwestern University Press.

Miller, P. C. 1986. "A Dubious Twilight": Reflections on Dreams in Patristic Literature. *Church History* 55(2): 153-164.

Mindell, A. 1982. *Dreambody: The Body's Role in Revealing the Self.* London: Routledge and Kegan Paul.

——— 1985. *Working with the Dream Body.* New York: Mathuen.

Moffitt, A., M. Kramer, and R. Hoffmann, eds. 1993. *The Functions of Dreaming.* Albany: State University of New York Press.

Moorcroft, W. 1993. *Sleep, Dreaming, and Sleep Disorders.* Second ed. Lanham, MD: University Press of America.

Morgan, W. 1932. Navaho Dreams. *American Anthropologist* 34: 390-405.

Moustakas, C. 1994. *Existential Psychotherapy and the Interpretation of Dreams.* Northvale, NJ: Jason Aronson.

Noll, R. 1994. *The Jung Cult: Origins of a Charismatic Movement.* Princeton, NJ: Princeton University Press.

Oberhelman, S. M., ed. 1991. *The Oneirocriticon of Achmet: A Medieval Greek and Arabic Treatise on the Interpretation of Dreams.* Lubbock: Texas Tech University Press.

O'Flaherty, W. D. 1984. *Dreams, Illusion, and Other Realities*. Chicago: University of
    Chicago Press.
O'Nell, C. W. 1976. *Dreams, Culture, and the Individual*. San Francisco: Chandler and
    Sharp.
Ong, R. K. 1985. *The Interpretation of Dreams in Ancient China*. Bochum, Germany:
    Studienverlag Brockmeyer.
Oppenheim, A. L. 1956. The Interpretation of Dreams in the Ancient Near East with a
    Translation of an Assyrian Dream-Book. *Transactions of the American
    Philosophical Society* 46(3): 179-343.
Palombo, S. R. 1978. *Dreaming and Memory: A New Information-Processing Model*. New
    York: Basic Books.
Parman, S. 1991. *Dream and Culture: An Anthropological Study of the Western Intellectual
    Tradition*. New York: Praeger.
Perls, F. 1970a. Dream Seminars. In *Gestalt Therapy Now*, edited by J. F. Shepherd and I.
    L. Shepherd. New York: Harper Colophon.
———— 1970b. Four Lectures. In *Gestalt Therapy Now*, edited by J. F. Shepherd and I. L.
    Shepherd. New York: Harper Colophon.
Piaget, J. 1962. *Play, Dreams, and Imitation in Childhood*. Translated by C. Gattegno and
    F. M. Hodgson. New York: W. W. Norton.
Radin, P. 1936. Ojibwa and Ottawa Puberty Dreams. In *Essays in Anthropology Presented
    to A. L. Kroeber*. Berkeley: University of California Press.
Rechtschaffen, A. 1978. The Single-Mindedness and Isolation of Dreams. *Sleep* 1: 97-109.
Reed, H. 1985. *Getting Help from Your Dreams*. Virginia Beach, VA: Inner Vision.
Roheim, G. 1952. *The Gates of the Dream*. New York: International Universities Press.
Rupprecht, C. S. 1990. Our Unacknowledged Ancestors: Dream Theorists of Antiquity, the
    Middle Ages, and the Renaissance. *Psychiatric Journal of the University of
    Ottawa* 15(2): 117-122.
———— ed. 1993. *The Dream and the Text: Essays on Language and Literature*. Albany:
    State University of New York Press.
———— 1996. Sex, Gender, and Dreams: From Polarity to Plurality. In *Among All These
    Dreamers: Essays on Dreaming and Modern Society*, edited by K. Bulkeley.
    Albany: State University of New York Press.
Rupprecht, C. S., and E. Lauter, eds. 1985. *Feminist Archetypal Theory: Interdisciplinary
    Revisions of Jungian Thought*. Knoxville: University of Tennessee Press.
Russo, R., ed. 1987. *Dreams Are Wiser Than Men*. Berkeley: North Atlantic Books.
Ryback, D., with L. Sweitzer. 1986. *Dreams that Come True*. New York: Ivy Books.
Rycroft, C. 1979. *The Innocence of Dreams*. New York: Pantheon.
Saint-Denys, H. 1982. *Dreams and How to Guide Them*. Translated by N. Fry. London:
    Duckworth.
Samuels, A. 1985. *Jung and the Post-Jungians*. Boston: Routledge and Kegan Paul.
Sanford, J. 1982. *Dreams: God's Forgotten Language*. New York: Crossroad.
Savary, L. M., P. H. Berne, and S. K. Williams. 1984. *Dreams and Spiritual Growth: A
    Christian Approach to Dreamwork*. Mahwah, NJ: Paulist Press.
Schneider, D. M., and L. Sharp. 1969. *The Dream Life of a Primitive People: The Dreams
    of the Yir Yoront of Australia*. Washington, DC: American Anthropological
    Association.

Schwartz-Salant, N., and M. Stein, eds. 1990. *Dreams in Analysis.* Wilmette, IL: Chiron.

Shafton, A. 1995. *Dream Reader: Contemporary Approaches to the Understanding of Dreams.* Albany: State University of New York Press.

Shweder, R. A. and R. A. LeVine. 1975. Dream Concepts of Hausa Children: A Critique of the "Doctrine of Invariant Sequence." *Ethos* 3: 209-230.

Siegel, A. B. 1990. *Dreams That Can Change Your Life.* Los Angeles: Jeremy Tarcher.

Signell, K. A. 1990. *Wisdom of the Heart: Working with Women's Dreams.* New York: Bantam Books.

Skura, M. 1981. *The Literary Use of the Psychoanalytic Process.* New Haven, CT: Yale University Press.

Smith, C. 1993. REM Sleep and Learning: Some Recent Findings. In A. Moffitt, M. Kramer, and R. Hoffmann (eds.), *The Functions of Dreaming.* Albany: State University of New York Press.

Spearing, A. C. 1976. *Medieval Dream-Poetry.* New York: Cambridge University Press.

Stairs, P., and K. Blick. 1979. A Survey of Emotional Content of Dreams Recalled by College Students. *Psychological Reports* 45: 839-842.

States, B. O. 1988. *The Rhetoric of Dreams.* Ithaca, NY: Cornell University Press.

———— 1993. *Dreaming and Storytelling.* Ithaca, NY: Cornell University Press.

———— 1994. Authorship in Dreams and Fictions. *Dreaming* 4(4): 237-254.

———— 1995. Dreaming "Accidentally" of Harold Pinter: The Interplay of Metaphor and Metonymy in Dreams. *Dreaming* 5(4): 229-246.

Stekel, W. 1943. *The Interpretation of Dreams: New Developments and Technique.* 2 vols. New York: Liveright.

Stephen, M. 1979. Dreams of Change: The Innovative Role of Altered States of Consciousness in Traditional Melanesian Religion. *Oceania* 50(1): 3-22.

Stern, P. J. 1976. *C. G. Jung: The Haunted Prophet.* New York: Delta.

Stewart, K. 1969. Dream Theory in Malaya. In *Altered States of Consciousness,* edited by C. Tart. New York: Harper Collins.

Stockholder, K. 1987. *Dream Works: Lovers and Families in Shakespeare's Plays.* Toronto: University of Toronto Press.

Tart, C., ed. 1969. *Altered States of Consciousness.* New York: Wiley.

Taylor, J. 1983. *Dream Work: Techniques for Discovering the Creative Power in Dreams.* Mahwah, NJ: Paulist Press.

———— 1992. *Where People Fly and Water Runs Uphill: Using Dreams to Tap the Wisdom of the Unconscious.* New York: Warner Books.

———— 1995. Debate on the Legacy of the Senoi. *ASD Newsletter* 12(2): 30-34.

Tedlock, B., ed. 1987. *Dreaming: Anthropological and Psychological Interpretations.* New York: Cambridge University Press.

———— 1991. The New Anthropology of Dreaming. *Dreaming* 1(2): 161-178.

Toffelmier, G., and K. Luomala. 1936. Dreams and Dream Interpretation of the Diegueno Indians of Southern California. *The Psychoanalytic Quarterly* 5: 195-225.

Tonay, V. 1990-1991. California Women and their Dreams: A Historical and Sub-Cultural Comparison of Dream Content. *Imagination, Cognition, and Personality* 10: 83-97.

Tonkinson, R. 1970. Aboriginal Dream-Spirit Beliefs in a Contact Situation: Jigalong, Western Australia. In *Australian Aboriginal Anthropology*, edited by R. M. Berndt. Sidney: University of Western Australia Press.

Trompf, G. W. 1990. *Melanesian Religion*. Cambridge, England: Cambridge University Press.

Ullman, M. 1994. The Experiential Dream Group: Its Application in the Training of Therapists. *Dreaming* 4(4): 223-230.

Ullman, M., and S. Krippner, with A. Vaughan. 1989. *Dream Telepathy: Experiments in Nocturnal ESP*. Second ed. Jefferson, NC: McFarland.

Ullman, M., and C. Limmer, eds. 1987. *The Varieties of Dream Experience*. New York: Continuum.

Ullman, M., and N. Zimmerman. 1979. *Working with Dreams*. Los Angeles: Jeremy Tarcher.

Urbina, S. P., and A. Grey. 1975. Cultural and Sex Differences in the Sex Distribution of Dream Characters. *Journal of Cross-Cultural Psychology* 6: 358-364.

Van de Castle, Robert. 1994. *Our Dreaming Mind*. New York: Ballantine.

Van der Post, L. 1975. *Jung and the Story of Our Time*. New York: Vintage.

Van Eeden, F. 1913. A Study of Dreams. *Proceedings of the Society for Psychical Research* 26: 431-461.

Van Meurs, J., with J. Kidd. 1988. *Jungian Literary Criticism, 1920-1980: An Annotated, Critical Bibliography of Works in English*. New York: Scarecrow Press.

Von Franz, M. L. 1986. *On Dreams and Death*. Boston: Shambhala.

——— 1991. *Dreams*. Boston: Shambhala.

Von Grunebaum, G. E., and R. Callois, eds. 1966. *The Dream and Human Societies*. Berkeley: University of California Press.

Wallace, A. F. C. 1958. Dreams and Wishes of the Soul: A Type of Psychoanalytic Theory Among the Seventeenth Century Iroquois. *American Anthropologist* 60: 234-248.

——— 1969. *The Death and Rebirth of the Seneca*. New York: Vintage.

Waterman, D., M. De Jong, and R. Magdelijns. 1988. Gender, Sex Role Orientation and Dream Content. In *Sleep '86*. New York: Gustav Fischer Verlag.

Wayman, A. 1967. Significance of Dreams in India and Tibet. *History of Religions* 7: 1-12.

Weidhorn, M. 1970. *Dreams in Seventeenth-Century English Literature*. Paris: Mouton.

Whitman, R., et al. 1962. The Dreams of the Experimental Subject. *Journal of Nervous and Mental Disease* 134: 431-439.

Whitmont, E. C., and S. B. Perera. 1989. *Dreams, a Portal to the Source*. New York: Routledge.

Williams, S. K. 1980. *Jungian-Senoi Dreamwork Manual*. Berkeley: Journey Press.

Wilmer, H. A. 1982. Vietnam and Madness: Dreams of Schizophrenic Veterans. *Journal of the American Academy of Psychoanalysis* 10: 47-65.

——— 1986. The Healing Nightmare: A Study of the War Dreams of Vietnam Combat Veterans. *Quadrant* 19(1): 47-61.

Wilson, D. B. 1993. *The Romantic Dream: Wordsworth and the Poetics of the Unconscious*. Lincoln: University of Nebraska Press.

Winget, C., and M. Kramer. 1979. *Dimensions of Dreams*. Gainesville: University Presses of Florida.

Wiseman, A. S. 1986. *Nightmare Help: For Children, From Children*. Berkeley: Ten Speed Press.

Wolman, B. B., ed. 1979. *Handbook of Dreams: Research, Theories, and Applications*. New York: Van Nostrand Reinhold.

Woods, R. L., and H. B. Greenhouse, eds. 1974. *The New World of Dreams*. New York: Macmillan.

Yamanaka, T., Y. Morita, and J. Matsumoto. 1982. Analysis of the Dream Contents in Japanese College Students by REM-Awakening Technique. *Folia Psychiatrica et Neurologica Japonica* 36: 33-52.

Zadra, A. L., D. C. Donderi, and R. O. Pihl. 1992. Efficacy of Lucid Dream Induction for Lucid and Non-Lucid Dreamers. *Dreaming* 2(2): 85-94.

Zepelin, H. 1980-1981. Age Differences in Dreams: I. Men's Dreams and Thematic Apperceptive Fantasy. *International Journal of Aging and Human Development* 12: 171-186.

——— 1981. Age Differences in Dreams: II. Distortion and Other Variables. *International Journal of Aging and Human Development* 13: 37-41.

Index

About the Author

KELLY BULKELEY, President of the Association for the Study of Dreams, teaches at Santa Clara University and is the author of several works on the subject of dreams.

ISBN 0-275-95889-2

90000>

EAN

HARDCOVER BAR CODE